THE
HORSE
AND
PONY
LOVER'S
ALMANAC

Joan Palmer

Eric Dobby Publishing

Published by Eric Dobby Publishing Ltd,
12 Warnford Road, Orpington, Kent BR6 6LW

A catalogue record of this book is available from
the British Library.

ISBN 1-85882 027 8

Typeset in Times by Kevin O'Connor
Printed and bound in Great Britain by
BPCC Hazell Books Ltd

CONTENTS

Dedications

Dedicated to my friends Hazel and Trish at
Raybrook Farm, Lynn at Laughton, near Lewes, who
rescues horses and ponies, and Kate and Michael
Lyster. But, above all, 'Dominus', 'Alexander',
'Galaxy', and Donkey, 'Eeyore', who gave endless
pleasure, and taught me so much.

JP

The author would like to thank Animal Photography
(Sally Anne Thompson and R.T. Willbie) for
allowing their beautiful horse and pony studies to
appear in this book.

INTRODUCTION

It is hard to recall any pastime that has afforded me so much pleasure as my association with the equine race, any hobby or sport that has resulted in my making so many friends as learning to ride has done.

The love of horses transcends the barriers of class, nationality and reserve, the mere mention of an interest in horses — albeit it made in the most unlikely circumstances — usually causing at least one companion to fumble eagerly in a wallet, bringing forth pictures of a horse or pony with all the eagerness of a parent showing off their first-born.

Some folk are lucky enough to be literally born in the saddle, growing up in a horsey environment, others have had doting parents who paid for riding lessons, or obtained tuition in return for doing jobs like grooming and mucking-out at a local stables.

Riding of course is by no means a pleasure confined to the young. Business executives and housewives take to the saddle and so do those well past their prime — often at their doctor's suggestion, because riding, like the proverbial apple a day, is good for you.

Every rider wants to have a horse of their own and study of the breeds in the Almanac should assist them in making a sound choice bearing in mind that only sturdy, native types such as mountain and moorland breeds can be kept out at grass all year round, finer boned steeds needing stabling, certainly from October through until May, while the section on Stable Management should answer any questions readers may have on the various types of livery available if they do not have a stable and/or paddock of their own.

And, even if owning your own mount must remain a dream, there is no reason why you should not enrol for a course of riding lessons at a local stables, whatever your age or circumstances, thereby ensuring that you have a personal Passport to Pleasure.

THE EVOLUTION OF THE HORSE

The most distant, recognisable ancestor of the horse, the Eohippus, a word taken from Greek words, meaning Dawn Horse, lived in North America more than 50 million years ago.

The Eohippus was small and wolf-like. It had sharp teeth, four toes on each foot, and a fox-like tail. In fact it had much in common with the early Rhinoceros and is believed to have evolved from the same primitive stock.

Eohippus was a forest and swamp dweller but, as time went on, and its habitat was replaced by pasture-land, it adapted to its changed environment. It developed deep-rooted teeth which were better equipped to grind and to obtain the most nutriment from sparse grazing; its legs became longer, making it speedier and better able to run from its enemies and as its weight became centred on its middle toe the others gradually disappeared through disuse.

Horses were first domesticated in Russia, some 6000 years ago, when they were kept mainly for food purposes, but they were put to work by the Sumerians in around 3500 BC pulling war chariots in Babylonia.

Horses range in size from Shetland ponies — the only difference between a horse and a pony is in size (an equine over 14.2hh is a horse) — to the lofty Hunter or Shire.

However, the oldest known variety is reckoned to be the Przevalski or Mongolian wild horse. Spotted horses too, such as the Appaloosa, have an ancient history and are depicted in Chinese paintings made more than 3000 years ago.

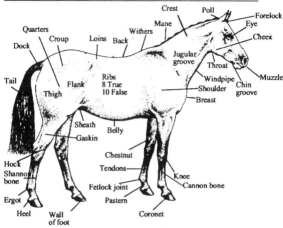

Points of the Horse

The points of the horse are the names given to the various parts of the body for ease of identification. Those most commonly in use are:

Belly Stomach

Cannon bone Shin bone. The foreleg bone below the knee, which ends at the fetlock.

Coronet The coronary band that surrounds the top of the foot at lower extremity of the growth of hair.

Crest The ride along the back of the neck, where mane grows.

Dock The part of the tail on which the hair grows.

Fetlock Tuft of hair behind fetlock joints, i.e. that which lies at the lower extremity of the cannon bone, adjoining pastern.

Forelock Section of mane that hangs over the forehead.

Hamstring Tendon running down the rear part of the second thigh to the point of the hock.

Hock The equivalent of the human ankle.

Chestnut Small horny protuberance on inside of all four legs. (Also the chestnut colour.)

Mane	Hair on the back of the horse's neck.
Quarters	Area lying between the rear of the flank and the root of the tail.
Pastern	Part of horse's leg lying between the fetlock joint and the coronet.
Second thigh	Also known as the Gaskin. That part of the hind limb above the hock that extends upwards to the stifle.
Stifle	That which would be termed a human knee. The junction of the tibia and the patella.
Shanks	see **Cannon bone**.
Shannon bone	Cannon bone of the horse's hind leg.
Sheath	Loose fold of skin in front of the scrotum.
Tendons	Fibrous structures forming bands and cords that attach the muscles to the bones of the horse's legs.
Withers	That part of the horse which commences at the base of the crest, sloping gradually into the back.

Horse and Pony Breeds

American Saddlebred

(Kentucky Saddlebred)

Character: Adaptable, friendly, intelligent.

History and origin: Developed by Kentucky pioneers from the best stock available, including the English thoroughbred, English 'amblers' and the Morgan. The founder of the existing type is reckoned to be the thoroughbred 'Denmark', foaled 1839, but it is a son of 'Denmark' which is the 'official' foundation stallion. The Saddlebred was much favoured by American Generals in the Civil War.

Looks: Colour usually bay, chestnut or grey. This is a light, elegant horse, the general appearance of which should indicate breeding and brilliance. It should have a long, arched neck, well sloped shoulders, round barrel, flat croup, and good, clean legs.

Size: 15hh—16hh.

Uses: Mainly a show animal renowned for its gaits — not merely the walk, trot and canter, but paces such as the running walk, stepping pace (slow rack) and fast rack. The head is flexed, neck and tail arched, the latter being achieved by nicking the muscles of the dock. Also makes a good harness horse.

Observations: Nicking and docking is illegal in the United Kingdom.

Pros and Cons: Not readily available outside the USA.

American Shetland Pony

Character: Affectionate, intelligent and lively.

History and origin: Developed in the United States from imported European stock.

Looks: Most colours acceptable. Taller and somewhat lighter than its European forebears.

Size: 10hh and no more than 11.2hh.

Uses: Much favoured for harness work and showing in hand. Its gait is similar to that of a hackney.

Observations: Tough. May be kept at grass. Has incredible strength in comparison to its weight and size.

Pros and Cons: Popular as a child's riding pony, show pony, and often as an adult's pet. But it can be wilful!

Andalucian

Character: Excellent temperament.

History and origin: Bred in Spain since 1571 when Philip II established stables at Cordoba, in the province of Andalucia, and developed the variety through crossings of native Iberian horses with the Barb. The Barb head has been retained despite subsequent crossings with English and French stock.

Christopher Columbus took a number of Andalucians with him on his voyage to the New World.

Looks: Colour is usually grey, but may be bay, black or roan. It is a powerful, well-bodied horse with short, straight back and prominent withers. It has a convex-shaped face, big, thoughtful eyes, small ears with the tips turned outwards, and it boasts a long and generous mane and tail.

Size: Approximately 15.2hh.

Uses: Traditional Spanish High School and Bull-fighting horse. Also used for dressage and jumping.

Observations: Famed for its frisky, high stepping gait.

Pros and Cons: Elegant. Great fun to ride. Just the mount for leading a procession.

Anglo-Arab

Character: The best attributes of Arab and Thoroughbred.

History and origin: The Anglo Arab has derived through crossing the Arab and the Thoroughbred. However, while in the United Kingdom the cross must be an Arab stallion and Thoroughbred mare or vice-versa, with no other alien blood whatsoever, the minimum percentages vary throughout the world. In the United States, for instance, an Anglo Arab would be required to have not less than 25 per cent Arab, and no more than 75 per cent Thoroughbred blood.

Looks: Colour is usually grey, but can be any solid horse colour. It has the Arab head and tail carriage, a short back, deep body, and strong quarters.

Size: Varies. Generally up to 16hh.

Uses: Dressage horse, hack, hunter, point to pointer, show jumper.

Observations: The Anglo Arab is generally regarded as a cross between two separate breeds. Only in France (see **French Anglo Arab**) is it regarded as a true breed.

Pros and Cons: A lively horse of brilliance and beauty, suited to the competitive and/or experienced rider.

13

French Anglo Arab

Character: The best attributes of Arab and Thoroughbred

History and origin: Developed in France from Anglo Arabs with an early infusion of blood from oriental type mares.

Looks: (See the **Anglo Arab**).

Size: Usually no more than 15.3hh but may attain 16hh.

Uses: Originally a popular cavalry horse but was subsequently bred for racing and also used for High School work and as a competition horse.

Observations: The French Anglo Arab is divided into two categories, the Anglo Arab and the Anglo Arab de Complement. The latter has to have less than 25 per cent pure Arab blood.

Pros and Cons: Fast and agile, the Anglo Arab of France is brave, beautiful and ideally suited to the ambitious, competitive rider.

Polish Anglo Arab (Polish Half Breed)

Character: Good temperament, powers of endurance and versatility.

History and origin: It was the Poles' intent to produce a horse which, unlike the heavy Percherons and Shires, would be capable of travelling to distant railway stations bearing in mind the sub-standard roads of the 1930s. This they did by developing a horse with English Thoroughbred and Arab and/or Anglo Arab blood.

Looks: Any known horse colour. This is a quality horse with deep girth, strong legs and good bone.

Size: Medium.

Uses: Cavalry horse, farm work, show jumping and general pleasure riding.

Observations: Types vary according to conditions and requirements. Those in Pomerania are based on the English Thoroughbred with the introduction of both local stock and German Trakehner brood mares, in the Kielce province from Arab stock, and in Warsaw and Lodz using English and Arab half breds.

Pros and Cons: Brave, fiery horse with looks and ability.

Kabardin (Russia) and Anglo Kabardin

Character: Gentle, sensitive. Lively, with strong powers of endurance.

History and origin: Indigenous to the mountain regions of the Caucasus and prized by nomadic tribesmen, the Kabardin's ancestry traces to crossings of native Mongol mares with stallions of Persian and Arab blood.

Looks: Colours are bay, dark bay, black and grey. Long head. Ears with tips pointing inwards. Short, muscular neck. Short, straight back. Powerful limbs with good bone. Generous flowing mane.

Size: 14.2hh—15.1hh.

Uses: Saddle, harness and pack horse. Endurance riding.

Observations: Crossed with the Thoroughbred the Anglo-Kabardin is produced. It is faster, taller and somewhat slighter than the Kabardin.

Pros and Cons: A sure footed, sensitive horse, ideal for mountainous country yet adaptable to its surroundings. You can't get lost with a Kabardin. It has an uncanny sense of direction!

Anglo Norman

Character: Strong, powerful, versatile.

History and origin: The foundations of the Anglo Norman lie in the powerful Norman war horse, examples of which came to England with William the Conqueror. The Norman did much to improve existing stock but its quality was subsequently spoilt through crossings with Danish and Mecklenburg cart horses. An infusion of Arab and Thoroughbred blood from 1775, and that of Norfolk trotters a century later, resulted in light carriage horses and racing trotters.

Looks: Good bone, strong muscle.

Size: 15.2hh—17hh.

Uses: Army horse, racing trotters, carriage horses. General purpose.

Observations: There are two types of Anglo Norman, the draught type which has Percheron and Boulonnais blood and the sporting type which is known as the Cheval de Selle Francais.

Pros and Cons: Fine horse. But watch out for those that are an unfortunate combination of conflicting types.

Note: (see also **French Trotters**)

Appaloosa

Character: Gentle animal that appreciates being a friend of the family. Seems able to assess its rider's capabilities. Good with children and other animals.

History and origin: Originated as war horses of the Nez Percé Indians in the Palouse region of Idaho. Took many years to re-establish after virtual annihilation by the United States Cavalry.

Looks: Most popular is the Leopard pattern, chocolate or black spots on basic white coat, but there are other patterns including snowflake, white spots on a dark background, or a self colour with spotted rump.

The skin is normally pink with grey mottling. Hooves are striped (particoloured). The tail and mane are generally wispy.

Size: 14.2hh—15.2hh.

Uses: Undertakes a multitude of tasks from quiet hacking to hunting, jumping, polo and performing in a circus.

Observations: A good doer. May be stabled or kept at grass.

Pros and Cons: An extremely versatile horse without any drawbacks — except that it stands out in a crowd, and seems to thrive on admiration.

Arab

Character: Gentle, but lively. Highly strung.

History and origin: The Arab is the oldest pure bred horse in the world. It is known to have existed long before Christ. Likenesses of Arab horses were depicted in the tombs of the Pharaohs. Bones of these horses, dating back 5,000 years, have been found in Iran.

The breed is known in the Arab world as Kehailan — pure bred. Every Thoroughbred registered in the United Kingdom has Arab blood in its veins.

Looks: Colours are predominantly chestnut and, occasionally, grey. Very occasionally black or brown. (Chestnut with three white feet is desired.) Head, small and tapering, very broad in forehead; large wide open eyes; short, level back; long, sloping shoulders, broad quarters; legs described as hard as iron.

Size: 14.2hh—15hh.

Uses: Racing, showing, pleasure riding.

Observations: Moslems believe that the Arab was created by Allah. Christians claim that Baz, the great grandfather of Noah, was the first man to capture and tame the Arab horse.

Pros and Cons: Ownership of the Arab is greatly desired, but remember that it is skittish and not for the novice.

Polish Arab

Character: Gentle, highly strung, intelligent.

History and origin: (See the **Arab** horse)

The Arab horse has played an important part in Polish horse breeding since the 16th century when Sigismund II kept a stud of pure white Arabians at Knyszyn. The Poles, who have a reputation as great horsemen, had a policy of introducing only fresh Arab blood straight from the desert.

Two of the largest Arab studs belong to the Sanguszko family. It was Jerome Sanguszko who organised the first expeditions from Europe to Arabia in 1803 to obtain bloodstock.

Looks: Colours (see the **Arab**). Good front, well set back, shoulders, short back, deep set body, short legs — to which have been added the Arabian air of elegance.

Size: 14.1hh—15hh.

Uses: Showing, jumping, racing. General purpose riding.

Observations: Polish Arabs are in demand all over the world. Some studs in the United States have been founded on imported Polish stock.

Pros and Cons: Highly desired horse that has made its mark internationally.

Ardennais (Ardennes)

Character: Amenable. Hardy. Willing worker.

History and origin: A breed that can claim either French or Belgian nationality depending on that part of the mountains, between the two countries, from which it comes.

It is an extremely ancient breed and has been through many changes. Most notable is its increased weight and size brought about through crossings with Brabançons to the detriment of many qualities, including energy and action.

The breed is alleged to have been bred in the Ardennes for more than 2,000 years and it is thought that, in the eighth century, Arab blood was introduced to give agility and style.

Looks: Colours are bay, dark liver, chestnut and roan. Generally of heavy draught type.

Size: 15.1hh—16.1hh. (There still exists in the mountains a smaller type (14.2hh—15.1hh) and this more closely resembles the original.)

Uses: Former cavalry horse and artillery wheeler. Farm worker.

Observations: Hardy horse with ability to withstand variable climatic conditions. Should have a good, free moving gait and is renowned for its working ability, even when on poor keep.

Pros and Cons: Numbers are diminishing as the demand for farm horses lessens.

Avelignese

Character: Good natured and reliable with great powers of endurance.

History and origin: A draught horse of ancient origin bred in northern and central Italy. There are a number of theories as to its ancestry, one being that it was abandoned in the Tyrolean valleys in 555 AD by the Ostrogoths as they fled from Byzantine armies. This suggestion would account for its Arab head and profile. The foundation stallion of the present type was 'Folie' (1874), which had been sired by an Arab stallion, El Bedaui XXII, out of a local mare.

Looks: Colour is usually golden chestnut with a flaxen mane and tail. It has an Arab head, a short, straight back that is both broad and muscular, short legs, well developed and muscular.

Size: 13.3hh—14hh.

Uses: Draught work, pleasure riding and pony trekking.

Observations: (See the **Haflinger**)

Pros and Cons: Worth its weight in gold as a trekking pony. An ideal novice ride.

Akhal Teke (Russia)

Character: Gentle, intelligent, speedy. Has great powers of endurance.

History and origin: Horse of great beauty and stamina bred by tribesmen in Turkmenistan to withstand extremes of temperature in desert conditions.

Whether the Akhal Teke descended from the Turkoman horse from Iran or vice versa is not known, but there is a distinct resemblance between the two breeds. However, the Akhal Teke has been pure bred for more than 4,000 years and was one of the first Russian horses to have its own Stud Book.

Looks: Colours are usually bay, grey and a shade of gold with black points. It has good bone and carriage, a Persian head, long neck, and beautiful soul-searching eyes.

Size: 14.3hh—15.2hh.

Uses: Former charger. Racing, show jumping and general pleasure riding.

Observations: Has considerable stamina. Weaklings were not permitted to survive.

Pros and Cons: Very fast. Imports have adapted well.

Alter Real

Character: Athletic and intelligent High School horse.

History and origin: This is the Portuguese national breed, a saddle horse with Spanish (Andalucian) blood).

In the mid 18th century, the heyday of High School work in the European courts, a Royal Stud was established in Alentejo. Three hundred Andalucian mares were imported as foundation stock. The resultant progeny showed the same abilities for exhibition work as those practised by the Lipizzaners at the Spanish Riding School in Vienna. Today the Portuguese Government promotes the breeding of the Alter Real.

Looks: Colours are usually bay, brown or grey. In appearance the horse is similar to the Andalucian with the same convex face, eyes set wide apart, and crested muscular neck. Its body is short and deep with powerful, muscular quarters.

Size: 15hh—15.3hh.

Uses: High School work. Demonstrating advanced equitation.

Observations: High stepping horse greatly prized by skilled Portuguese horsemen.

Pros and Cons: A joy to watch — and to ride if you are up to it!

American Miniature Horse

Character: Gentle nature. Intelligent. Quiet.

History and origin: (See the **Falabella**) The breed was developed by the Falabella family on the Recreo de Roca Ranch in Argentina.

Looks: Any known horse colour. However the Appaloosa coat patterns are greatly desired.

Size: Less that 8.2hh.

Uses: Mainly kept as pets, but can be put into harness.

Observations: While the English Studs have received considerable publicity and the English Thoroughbred has played its part, the variety is also gaining popularity in North America.

It should be noted that the gestation period of these small horses is thirteen months, two months longer than any other breed of horse.

Pros and Cons: A delightful pet, but do remember that it is far too delicate to be ridden, is likely to be expensive, and that it requires good feed and stabling in winter.

Boulonnais

Character: Heavy draught horse of considerable stamina.

History and origin: A heavy horse bred in France during the Crusades and greatly improved by an infusion of blood from Arab and Barb stallions brought from the East by French Crusaders.

Looks: Colours are bay, black, blue roan, red roan and dappled grey. It is quick to mature and has great bone and muscle. There are two types, the Abbeville, of medium size, and the Dunkirk, which is very large and heavy.

Size: 16hh—17hh.

Uses: Farm and/or industrial work. One of its tasks used to be to convey French oysters from the seashore.

Observations: Reckoned — with the Dutch Draught — to be 'the strongest, most impressive horse in Europe'.

Pros and Cons: Surprisingly gentle for its weight and size.

Brabant

Also known as **Brabançon** and **Flemish Draught**

Character: Good temperament and strong constitution. A willing worker.

History and origin: A descendant of the Flanders horse of medieval times developed in low-lying country in Belgium rich in fertile soil and herbage.

At one time there were three varieties, the Big Horse of the Dendre, the Grey Horse of Nivelles, and the immense sized Horse of Mehaignc, but these have not been recognised since the beginning of the twentieth century. Brabants are also bred in the Gorki Province of Russian while those exported to England are believed to have had an influence on the Shire.

Looks: Usually red roan with black points. A horse of great weight and power with massive shoulders and quarters. Its head is square in shape and it has a short, deep body.

Size: 16hh—17hh.

Uses: Once the mount of Knights in armour and thereafter a willing farm worker, its use, due to mechanisation, is now dwindling.

Observations: A horse of strength, weight and tractability.

Pros and Cons: Not only very docile but described 'as the most powerful living tractor in the world'.

Breton

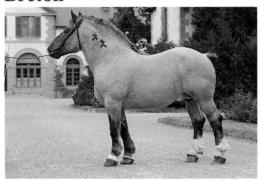

Character: Strong. Adaptable. Willing.

History and origin: The Breton has been bred for many centuries in the poor land of Brittany.

There are three distinct types: the heavy draught, the draught post, and the mountain draught horse.

Looks: Colours may be bay roan, black, chestnut, grey, or strawberry roan.

It has a well proportioned head, short, straight back, broad, muscular withers - not too pronounced - and short, muscular limbs with some feathering.

Size: Heavy draught: 15.2hh—16.2hh.

Draught post: 15hh—16hh

Mountain draught: up to 14.2hh

Uses: Farm and coaching work.

Observations: Hardy and able to survive on poor keep.

Pros and Cons: A willing work horse.

Camargue

Character: Quiet, Great powers of endurance.

History and origin: The 'Wild horses of the sea' are of ancient origin, thought to descend from the Solutrean 'ram-headed horse', the prototype of the modern Barb.

Reputed to have been admired by Julius Caesar, the breed has undoubtedly benefited from an infusion of Arab and Barb blood.

Looks: Colour is almost always grey, but can be bay and brown. Largish head with straight or convex profile; short, broad ears; short, straight body, prominent withers; fairly short legs. Large, very expressive eyes.

Size: 13.1hh—15hh.

Uses: This is the horse on which French Cowboys work the famous black fighting bulls in the Camargue.

Observations: Lives in herds in wild state and seems impervious to cold. Makes a quiet, reliable riding and/or pack pony, once tamed.

Pros and Cons: Nicknamed 'Crin Blanc' (white hair), this is a breed which, while slow to mature, often lives to a ripe old age.

Canadian Quarter Horse

Character: Combines good disposition with keen intelligence. Gentle enough to be entrusted with children's safety, but with plenty of 'get up and go'.

History and origin: Developed in Canada from American Quarter horse stock. (See the **American Quarter Horse**.)

Looks: Colours vary from black and chestnut to dun, grey and Palomino. Sturdy, powerfully built horse, with very well developed hind quarters. Alert intelligence reflected by short, broad head, topped by little 'foxy' ears, wide set, kind eyes, sensitive nostrils, short muzzle and firm mouth.

Size: 15.2hh—16.1hh.

Uses: See entry the **American Quarter Horse**. But also used extensively, in Canada, for the Rodeo.

Observations: Easy to keep, thrifty and robust.

Pros and Cons: Ideal, versatile 'friend of the family'. Easy to train. Fast.

Caspian

Character: Gentle, intelligent pony of great versatility.

History and origin: More of a miniature horse than a pony. Believed to be one of the forerunners of the Arab.

Although known to have been tamed by the Mesopotamians in 3000 BC the variety was thought to be extinct until 1965 when a few bedraggled examples were discovered on the northern shores of Iran bordering the Caspian Sea.

Looks: Colours are bay, chestnut or grey, (very occasionally with white markings on the head and legs). The head is small with tapering muzzle; large eyes, wide nostrils; short, straight back, slightly pronounced withers; well-boned legs.

Size: 9.2hh—11.2hh.

Uses: Children's pony, jumping, harness work.

Observations: Fast, narrow backed pony with great powers of acceleration.

Pros and Cons: Proud looking pony of immense ability.

Cleveland Bay

Character: Gentle horse of stamina and style.

History and origin: A horse of great antiquity which is almost indigenous to the County of Yorkshire in England. It has, for more than a century, been described as 'probably the nearest to a fixed type as any breed in England'. But there were still two types — one designed for coaching, the other for agriculture.

Looks: Always a whole bay colour.

The body is wide and deep, not long, but strong with muscular limbs. The head is rather large, but well carried on a long, thin neck. Loins, strong and muscular, legs clean. Essentially with very sound, hard blue feet.

Size: 16hh—16.2hh.

Uses: Mainly used these days for mating with Thoroughbreds to produce fine hunters.

Observations: Renowned as a coach and procession horse; also as a farm worker.

Pros and Cons: Capable of doing the work demanded of all heavy breeds.

Clydesdale

Character: Docile. A combination of weight, size and activity.

History and origin: A native of Lanarkshire (once known as Clydesdale) in Scotland. Traces back to the middle of the 18th century when, through the use of imported Flemish stallions, native stock was upgraded to meet trade demand for animals of more weight and substance. By the middle of the 19th century, following infusion of Flemish and Friesian blood, the Clydesdale was firmly established.

Looks: Preferably bay or brown with a white stripe on the face, white stockings on legs up to, and over, the knees and hocks. The Clydesdale combines quality and size without grossness and bulk. It has exceptionally sound feet and limbs.

Size: About 16.2hh.

Uses: Originally used to transport coal from the mines and subsequently for farm work, later coming into its own as a coaching horse. Still used as a dray horse for breweries.

Observations: An active animal in need of regular exercise.

Pros and Cons: High prices are obtained for show winners. The breed is much in demand for export.

Cob

Character: It is, or should be, a 'perfect gentleman'.

History and origin: The Cob is not a breed, but a type, a big-bodied, 'stuffy' horse, much favoured as a comfortable ride by the portly, elderly gentleman or nervous beginner.

Many Cobs have Welsh cob ancestry but there are those with cart horse and the like in their background.

Looks: Colours are generally bay, black, brown, chestnut or grey. The Cob has a short back and great girth. Its 'quality' head is set on a neck which is arched and elegant. The tail was traditionally docked. Since 1949 this practise has been illegal in the United Kingdom. Now the Cob's tail is carried high and with gaiety. The mane is hogged.

Size: No more than 15.3hh.

Uses: Hacking. Hunting.

Observations: Up to weight.

Pros and Cons: Not so easy to fall off as the more racy types.

Connemara

Character: Docile, sound, intelligent.

History and origin: Indigenous to that part of Connaught in the West of Ireland, known as Connemara. Some say its ancestry traces back to horses which swam ashore from a wreck of the Spanish Armada in 1588, but it is more widely thought that the pony was in Connemara even before that time and that it owes the obvious infusion of Arab and Spanish blood to one time trading between Spain and Galway, its beginnings being not dissimilar to that of the Highland pony with possibly oriental ancestry.

Looks: The predominant colour is grey, but Connemaras are also black, bay, brown and, occasionally, dun, roan and Palomino. Compact body, short legs, well sloped shoulders, small, well balanced head, and a generous mane and forelock.

Size: 13hh—14.2hh.

Uses: Child's riding pony, hunting, jumping, works well in harness.

Observations: Tough, native pony with great staying power. Can be kept at grass and seems to thrive upon poor keep.

Pros and Cons: Versatile and friendly. Cast iron constitution.

Criollo

Character: Has great powers of endurance.

History and origin: The Criollo is the native horse of Argentina. It is a descendant of Andalucian and Barb horses brought to South America by the Conquistadores.

It is understood that many of these horses escaped and lived wild for a considerable time thus building up their renowned resistance to disease and the ability to survive under adverse conditions.

Looks: Colours range from dun to black, roan and skewbald. Compact and sturdy, the Criollo has a fairly long head and neck. It has a short, straight back, pronounced withers and muscular legs.

Size: 14hh—15hh.

Uses: Hacking. Endurance riding.

Observations: In Brazil there is a smaller type, the Crioulo and, in Venezuela, one of slighter build, the Llanero.

Pros and Cons: Famed for their remarkable endurance on 'Tschiffley's ride' (a 13,350 mile trek from Buenos Aires to New York). Also made its contribution to the Argentinian Polo pony through crossing with the Thoroughbred.

Dales

Character: Hardy, intelligent and sound.

History and origin: A native of the eastern side of the North of England. In fact, the Dales pony came from the East, the Fells pony from the West and, at one time, it was impossible to distinguish between the two. Nowadays the Dales is larger due to the introduction of Clydesdale blood.

Looks: Colours are bay, black or brown. Neat, pony head; deep, compact body, somewhat straight shoulders and an abundance of fine hair on the heels.

Size: 13.2hh—14.2hh.

Uses: Driving, general pleasure riding, jumping and trekking.

Observations: Used to transport lead to the Docks from mines in Northumbria.

Pros and Cons: It has been suggested that the Dales' straight shoulders made it more suitable to drive than to ride. Nonetheless it is a firm favourite with Pony Club members.

Dartmoor Pony

Character: Brave, docile and hardy.

History and origin: Indigenous to Dartmoor in the Southwest of England. Breed members are still to be found there, living wild under adverse conditions.

Looks: Colours are generally bay, black and brown, but may be any horse colour with the exception of piebald and skewbald.

Head well set on; strong neck; well muscled back, loins and hind-quarters.

Size: 12hh—12.2hh.

Uses: Excellent child's pony.

Observations: Can carry a surprising amount of weight for their size.

Pros and Cons: Long lived. Often handed down through the family.

Døle Pony

Character: Powerful pony of good temperament and considerable stamina.

History and origin: Possibly derived in antiquity from the same stock as the Dales and Fell which it strongly resembles, the Døle or Døle Gudbrandsal has existed for centuries in the Gudbrandsal Valley in Norway.

Looks: Colours are bay, black, brown, grey and, very occasionally, dun. Similar in looks to the Dales and Fell with small, pony head.

Size: 14.2hh—15.2hh.

Uses: Draught, pleasure riding and trotting. Still used to transport timber in its native land.

Observations: There is some variation in type, the lighter pony having Thoroughbred influence and being much sought after for its trotting ability.

Pros and Cons: Useful all rounder.

Don

Character: Gentle and steady, but lively.

History and origin: Russian Steppe horse which traces back to the 18th century when the original small, sturdy Don horse, bred in the Don Valley, was much improved by the introduction of Karabakh, Turkmene and Karabair blood. More recently the Orlov and the English Thoroughbred have made a contribution to this fine, Russian saddlehorse.

Looks: Colours are bay, black, brown, chestnut and grey. The Don has a ram-like head, long, straight back, prominent withers and long, muscular legs.

Size: 15.1hh—15.3hh.

Uses: Saddlehorse, light draught.

Observations: Has considerable powers of endurance. Used by the Cossacks in 1812 against Napoleon's Army.

Pros and Cons: Prized in its native land where it is used to improve many breeds, and in the development of new ones, such as the Budyonny.

Donkey

Character: Gentle, determined, intelligent and loyal.

History and origin: The domesticated donkey is a descendant of the Wild African Ass which was bred and tamed long before the horse. It was introduced into the British Isles as a pack animal by the Roman Legions and was referred to as a common Ass until the 18th century.

Looks: By no means always grey. Donkeys may be brown, dun, ginger and a pink shade — which in a horse would be called strawberry roan. Also white and what is called broken coloured, that is, without the customary cross on its back. Neat head in proportion to body, level back, deep girth, limbs straight and true.

Size: Average 10hh (less for miniatures). In the United Kingdom donkeys measuring between 10.2hh and 12hh are known as large standards. Spanish and American donkeys are bigger.

Uses: Usually associated with carrying laundry baskets in the East. However the donkey is fast gaining a following elsewhere as a first class pet, child's mount, showing and driving animal.

Observations: Susceptible to pneumonia so must have a stable or field shelter.

Pros and cons: Lives for donkey's years — 37 is average. Also appreciates a companion of its own kind.

Dutch Draught

Character: Active, docile, brave and willing.

History and origin: Traces back to the second half of the last century via the Stud Books of the Royal Netherlands Draught Horse Society.

Zeeland mares were crossed with Belgian heavy draughts and Ardennese stallions resulting in what is probably the most massive, heavily muscled horse bred in the western world.

Looks: Colours are bay, black, chestnut and grey. Short neck, powerfully muscled front. massive, well developed forequarters, wide, heavy powerful hind quarters and strong, muscular legs.

Size: Up to 16.3hh.

Uses: Draught horse. Exhibition purposes.

Observations: Matures early and lives long. Considerable powers of endurance.

Pros and Cons: Has a long, active working life and fares well even when on poor keep.

Dutch Warmblood

Character: Of docile and willing temperament.

History and origin: Traces back to two long established Dutch breeds, the Groningen and the Gelderland with infusions of blood from the English Thoroughbred and other fine European riding horses. The blood of Lipizzaner stallions was introduced as recently as the 1980s. However the Dutch Warmblood Stud Book was opened as long ago as 1958.

Looks: Any solid horse colours. Well proportioned head, pronounced withers, straight back, strong, muscular legs.

Size: 15.3hh—16.3hh.

Uses: Saddle horse, show jumping, dressage and light draught.

Observations: Some of these horses have become internationally acclaimed for both jumping and dressage.

Pros and Cons: A useful and thoroughly likable all rounder.

Dulmen

Character: Somewhat wild and independent. Strong powers of endurance.

History and origin: The Dulmen is Germany's only native, wild pony, with the exception of the Senner which once inhabited the Teutoberg forest of Hanover and is now believed to be extinct. The Dulmen have lived in a semi-wild state in the Meerfelder Bruch in Westphalia since 1316. The property of the Duke of Croy, they are rounded up each year and sold.

Looks: Colours are bay, black, brown, chestnut, dun and roan. Small head, straight profile, long straight back, not particularly good formation. Legs are strong and well muscled.

Size: Approximately 12.2hh.

Uses: Nothing specific. Dulmen crossed with Arabs have become children's ponies.

Observations: Impervious to bad weather.

Pros and Cons: Becoming increasingly rare.

East Friesian

Character: Brave, strong, spirited.

History and origin: Prior to World War II, the East Friesian from East Germany and the Oldenburg from the West developed along similar lines with much cross breeding between the two. However when East and West were divided these horses progressed along individual lines.

In the case of the East Friesian, Arab blood was introduced and, latterly, that of the Hanoverian.

Looks: Colours are bay, black, brown, chestnut and grey. Well proportioned head, wide awake eyes, long, arched neck. Back, long and straight, broad deep chest, muscular legs.

Size: 15.2hh—16.1hh.

Uses: Saddlehorse, driving, light draught.

Observations: Gazai, a grey Arab stallion, is credited with greatly benefiting the East Friesian breed.

Pros and Cons: Handsome, all purpose horse.

Einsiedler

Character: Docile, useful, willing.

History and origin: Named after the town of Einsiedler in the Swiss Canton of Schwyz, the breed is known to have existed as long ago as 1064 although it did not reach its zenith until the 16th century.

Alas, following the French Revolution, the studs were looted and the breed diminished.

The Einsiedler now owes much to the introduction of Anglo-Norman blood and is often referred to as the Swiss Norman.

Looks: Colours are bay and chestnut. (For conformation see **Anglo-Norman/Selle Français**.)

Size: 15.3hh—16.2hh.

Uses: Pleasure riding, light draught.

Observations: Developed by Benedictine monks.

Pros and Cons: A favourite with the Swiss Army as a Competition and Show Jumping horse.

Eriskay

Character: Docile and sensitive. Hardy.

History and origin: This is the rarest British pony, the only surviving ancestor of the Hebrides pony indigenous to the Western Isles of Scotland. It has Norse connections and is likely to have had Celtic origins. Likenesses of the Eriskay are to be seen on Pictish headstones.

Looks: Colour is usually grey. Long face, with eyes set fairly wide apart; alert, kindly expression, small ears, generous forelock and mane; sturdy build.

Size: Approx 14hh.

Uses: Child's pony.

Observations: Ran wild in the early to mid 1800s. However most were subsequently crossbred. Those from the Isle of Skye were improved by the introduction of Arabian and Highland pony blood while those from Uish benefited from Arabian, Spanish, Clydesdale and Norwegian blood and, it is said, those from Barra by stolen Arabians.

Pros and Cons: A fine, hardy child's pony of good temperament. This is one of a number of breeds with low numbers on which the Rare Breeds Survival Trust are keeping a watchful eye.

Estonian

Character: Docile and obedient.

History and origin: The Estonian (or Klepper) is a little-known breed from the Baltic with an infusion of eastern blood.

Looks: Usually chestnut or bay this is a small horse with short legs, powerful feet, and a thick coat, sometimes with an eel stripe.

Size: Variable. Usually 13hh—15hh.

Uses: An influx of alien blood has resulted in a number of variations of this former wild horse which has adapted to the individual climate and conditions.

Observations: Harness horses. Good trotters and pacers.

Pros and Cons: Extremely hardy. Adaptable to extremes of climate.

Exmoor Pony

Character: Affectionate. Intelligent.

History and origin: Believed to be Britain's oldest native breed and to have pulled war chariots for the Celts, the Exmoor is recorded in the Domesday Book when, as now, it roamed the moors in herds. However all are privately owned.

Looks: Colours are brown, bay or dun, without any white markings. Head is rather long, ears short, chest deep and wide, back of medium length, with powerful loins; legs clean and straight. The fact that the shoulders are so well set back is the reason why this pony is invariably very sure footed.

Size: Not more than 12.2hh for a mare, 12.3hh for geldings and stallions.

Uses: The ideal children's pony.

Observations: Tough. May be kept at grass all year round.

Pros and Cons: Strong, courageous little pony that is just as tough — and as lovable — as it looks and which, because of its generous lifespan, is very often handed down through the family.

Falabella

Character: Friendly. Intelligent.

History and origin: Despite its small size, the Falabella is not a pony, but a miniature horse, bred by the Falabella family in Argentina; also by Lord and Lady Fisher at the Kilverstone Stud in Norfolk, England and by Toy Horse International in West Sussex, England.

In the 19th century, Senor Falabella's grandfather encountered an Indian's pony with what was described as 'dwarf sickness'. He bought the stallion and bred from it. It was found that the small stallion's genes for tiny offspring were dominant and that, when put to normal sized mares, the resultant progeny would be much smaller. Many breeds have been used and reproduced in a diminutive state.

Looks: Any type and colour. Well proportioned horse, in miniature, with fine bones and feet.

Size: Less than 7hh.

Uses: A delightful, if expensive, pet. Sometimes put in harness.

Observations: Rather delicate. Essential to rug up and/or stable in winter. Needs good feeding.

Pros and Cons: Definitely not strong enough to be ridden.

Fell

Character: Active, calm, docile and willing.

History and origin: Once identical to the Dales, which is now a larger animal, the Fell inhabits the Western side of the English Pennines.

Looks: Colours are bay, black, brown, chestnut, dun and grey, preferably without any white markings. Neat, pony head, solid, rather heavy body. Long, well-muscled legs, heels well feathered.

Size: Up to 14.2hh.

Uses: Like the Dales, the Fell used to transport lead from mines to the docks on Tyneside, travelling some 240 miles each week, carrying 16 stone in weight. Today it is a popular riding pony.

Observations: May well be descended from the extinct Galloway pony which inhabited the Scottish Border country. The Galloway was crossed with Friesians introduced by the Roman legions.

Pros and Cons: Tough. Sure-footed. A good all round choice.

Finnish

Character: Brave, docile, willing.

History and origin: The Finnish horse results from crossings of native stock with a variety of other breeds. There were two types, the Finnish Universal, not dissimilar to the present type, and the Finnish Draught, which was a heavier animal.

Looks: Colours are bay, black, brown, chestnut and grey. Fairly heavy head, small pointed ears, expressive eyes; fairly short back, deep chest, strong legs.

Size: Up to 15.2hh.

Uses: Speedy trotting horse. Pulls sleighs in its native land.

Observations: The modern Finnish horse is considered too light for draught work, but too heavy for a popular riding horse!

Pros and Cons: Sure footed and agile. Not often seen outside Finland.

Fjord

Character: Docile and willing.

History and origin: The Fjord is a native Norwegian pony of considerable quality, no doubt due to an infusion of Arab blood. It has been bred pure for centuries, but still bears some resemblance to the Przevalski, the oldest known wild breed of horse.

Looks: Colour is always between dun and cream with a dark dorsal stripe. Sturdy pony with medium sized back and strong hindquarters. Short, well-boned limbs, some feathering on heels.

Size: 13hh—14.2hh.

Uses: Pack pony, draught, riding.

Observations: The mane is traditionally clipped so as to stand up in a crest. Like its coat, the mane becomes less fluffy as the pony matures.

Pros and Cons: Excellent general purpose pony.

Frederiksborg

Character: Sound, strong, versatile.

History and origin: The Frederiksborg is one of the oldest, best known, Danish breeds. It takes its name from the Stud, north of Copenhagen, where it was bred.

The breed was developed there in 1562 by King Frederick II with the aim of producing a horse for the high school work at that time popular in the European courts.

Looks: Chestnut in colour this is a deep bodied horse with a large, plain head, straight face, and short, sturdy legs.

Size: Up to 16hh.

Uses: Cavalry, high school and harness work. Still used for agriculture in its homeland.

Observations: Of Andalucian/Neapolitan ancestry, the Frederiksborg was used, during the 18th century, to improve Lipizzaner stock.

Pros and Cons: Exceedingly rare.

Freiberger

Character: Gentle, strong and easily trained.

History and origin: The Freiberger is a warmblood horse, bred in the Jura mountains of western Switzerland, with a mixture of blood in its veins including that of the Norman and Anglo-Norman as well as Postier Breton and Arab Shagya from Hungary.

Looks: Most known horse colours. A light to middleweight, it is a compact, muscular horse with a small head, strong limbs and some feathering.

Size: 14.3hh—15.2hh.

Uses: Light draught. Bred to assist the Swiss Army in the Jura mountains. Also valued for farm work.

Observations: Sure footed with good action.

Pros and Cons: Strenuous efforts are being made by the Swiss National Stud to restrict outside influences and standardise conformation of this fine breed.

French Trotter

Character: Attractive and robust with considerable stamina.

History and origin: Developed in France in the 19th century to meet the needs of the growing sport of harness racing.

The foundation stock were British imports, notably a Norfolk trotter named 'The Norfolk Phenomenon' and an English Thoroughbred, 'The Heir of Lynne', which were crossed with Normandy mares, which in turn produced the Anglo-Norman.

Looks: Colours are bay, brown, chestnut and, very occasionally, grey. Conformation varies, some examples resembling the Thoroughbred, others a sturdier, old-fashioned type, but both have very strong hindquarters.

Uses: Harness racing. It is also a good general purpose horse.

Observations: The French Trotter and the Anglo-Norman (which became known as the Selle Français) were not regarded as a separate breed until the 20th century.

Pros and Cons: Probably the most robust trotter in the world. The best known studs are still based in Normandy.

Friesian

Character: Docile, strong and sensitive.

History and origin: The Friesian takes its name from Friesland in the North of Holland. The remains of horses, dating back to 1000 BC which were found in that area prove that it has changed little over the centuries. It was a favourite in medieval times for carrying men in armour — and for its trotting ability.

Looks: Black, sometimes with a white star on the forehead. It has a narrow head, short ears and expressive eyes. Short, straight back, broad chest and strong limbs. Its mane is plentiful and its legs have generous feathering often reaching up to the knee joint.

Size: Approx. 15hh.

Uses: Carriage horse. Saddle horse up to weight. Agricultural worker.

Observations: Improved in the Middle Ages by the introduction of Andalucian and Oriental blood.

Pros and Cons: A willing worker of pleasant disposition and versatility that is also a good doer.

Furioso

Character: Docile. Lively. Willing.

History and origin: Traces back to Hungarian mares of Nonius stock and, in particular, to two stallions imported from England towards the end of the 19th century to the stud at Mezohegyes after which it is named. The stallions, 'North Star', a Norfolk Trotter (1844) and 'Furioso', an English Thoroughbred (1836) sired two separate lines. These have now been channelled into one fine breed, the Furioso-North Star. The resultant progeny was distributed throughout the length and breadth of the Austrian Empire.

Looks: Colours are bay, black and brown. Well-proportioned head, generous mane, long, straight back, prominent withers, well-muscled legs.

Size: 16hh—16.2hh.

Uses: Sports horse, saddle horse, light draught.

Observations: Stress free with plenty of stamina. Makes a good competition horse.

Pros and Cons: Over the last 30 years Hanoverian blood has been added to improve sporting quality.

Gelderland

Character: Docile and willing.

History and origin: Originated from the Dutch province of Gelderland where it was crossed, long ago, with Anglo-Normans, Holsteins, Norfolk Trotters and English Thoroughbreds thus producing a fine farm horse. However as the need for agricultural work declined, efforts were made to refine it into a light draught and saddle horse.

Looks: Colours are usually chestnut or grey. This is a wide, deep horse with a powerful body, well-proportioned head and strong muscular legs.

Size: 15.2hh—16.1hh.

Uses: Farm, saddle and light draught.

Observations: Used as foundation stock in the development of the Dutch Warmblood.

Pros and Cons: This strong, handsome horse with stylish action is in danger of becoming extinct.

German Trotter

Character: Strong and willing with considerable stamina.

History and origin: Likely to have resulted from crossings of French and Orlov Trotters imported into German studs at the end of the 19th century.

Looks: Most known horse colours. Sturdy, well-proportioned animal with well muscled legs (see also **French Trotters**).

Size: Approximately 16hh.

Uses: Trotting, light draught.

Observations: It should be noted that all trotting breeds (see **French Trotters**) inherit this aptitude from Norfolk (English) Trotters and English Thoroughbreds.

Pros and Cons: The Americans lead the field in trotting races and only the French have managed to compete. However Germany and other European countries have developed their own breeding programmes. The Trotter's life is a hard one. It often has to enter several races in one day.

Gotland

Character: Elegant. Quiet, but lively.

History and origin: This pony has lived for many centuries on Gotland Island in the Baltic Sea — indeed it is believed to have altered little since the Stone Age. However, Oriental blood was added when two stallions were brought to the island in the 19th century.

Looks: Colours are usually bay or brown, but may be black, chestnut dun or Palomino. Light and elegant, the Gotland has a small head, straight face, with eyes set well apart and a full forelock; long, straight back, well-muscled legs.

Size: 12hh—14hh.

Uses: Child's pony, light draught, trotting races.

Observations: Still runs wild in the woods. Indeed the name Skogsruss, often attributed to it, means 'Little horse of the woods'.

Pros and Cons: A hardy, attractive animal which, since 1954 has been protected by the Swedish government.

Groningen

Character: Strong, docile and obedient.

History and origin: The Groningen is a Dutch farm horse which, like the Gelderland, has been in danger of extinction. Indeed it might have been lost for ever had not the Dutch taken steps to ensure its survival in the 1970s when only one stallion remained. The breed was developed on larger lines than the Gelderland by the introduction of Oldenburg and East Friesian blood, to which Suffolk Punch blood was added in the 19th century to give it the stamina needed for farm work.

Looks: Colours are bay, black, brown and dark brown. Strong back, deep body, long head, well-shaped limbs. Stylish action.

Size: 15.3hh—16.1hh.

Uses: Light draught. Saddle horse up to weight.

Observations: Has been used as foundation stock for the Dutch Warmblood.

Pros and Cons: Versatile horse which has a very refined head and neck, good conformation, excellent legs and feet and stylish action despite its weight.

Hack

Character: Well mannered, responsible, elegant.

History and origin: The word 'Hack' is an English one. One hires a Hack for pleasure riding — hacking — and the Hack, not to be confused with the Hackney (Harness horse), must be sound in wind and limb and quiet to ride.

Looks: Any recognised horse colour. Well balanced, usually with much of the Thoroughbred in its makeup.

Size: Hack (Show) Ladies. A horse exceeding 14.2hh but not exceeding 15hh.

Hack (Show) Small. Exceeding 14.2hh and not exceeding 15hh.

Hack (Show) Large. Exceeding 15hh but not exceeding 15.3hh.

Uses: Riding horse.

Observations: The Arab and Anglo Arab and indeed working ponies often contribute to the Hack, which must always have impeccable manners.

Pros and Cons: This is a horse one should be able to hire from a livery stable without any qualms.

Hackney Horse (USA)

Character: High spirited and showy.

History and origin: Descended from the Norfolk Trotter (and Roadster) which, some say, may have itself derived from Danish horses introduced into Britain in the 11th century and subsequently crossed with Thoroughbreds and Arabs. While the Hackney horse is generally attributed to England, a taller version is bred in the USA.

Looks: Colours are bay, black, brown, chestnut and, very occasionally, roan. Head is small, neat with straight profile and large eyes; back short and straight; chest wide and deep. Legs not too long and hind legs carried somewhat behind.

Size: In the USA may reach a height of 16.3hh (GB 15hh).

Uses: Light draught, saddle horse.

Observations: High stepping horse of good stamina. Brisk of movement.

Pros and Cons: Sturdy and generally long limbed.

Hackney Pony

Character: High spirited and showy.

History and origin: This is the show version of the Hackney horse with the Norfolk Trotter as an ancestor to which has been added an infusion of both Fell and Welsh pony blood which accounts for its small size. It was developed in the 19th century as a light draught pony.

Looks: Colours are usually bay, black and brown, (very rarely) chestnut. Neat head, long neck, strong shoulders, compact body and sturdy limbs.

Size: Under 14hh.

Uses: Show pony, usually driven rather than ridden.

Observations: Once a humble tradesman's delivery horse it is now much favoured by the gentry because of its elegant action.

Pros and Cons: Described as having the most extravagant action which it is possible to produce in a horse.

Haflinger

Character: Strong, sure footed and agile.

History and origin: Mountain pony credited with originating in the Tyrolean village of Hafling, and endowed with Arab blood. Aroused considerable German interest prior to the Second World War and its breeding was encouraged. Stallions are reared in the Central Stud at Piber, Austria.

Looks: Colour is chestnut with flaxen mane and tail, (sometimes Palomino). It has a long body, broad straight back, muscular quarters and short legs. It has a small, elegant Arab head.

Size: Average 14hh.

Uses: Pack and draught horse. Agriculture.

Pros and Cons: See also **Avelignese**.

Hanoverian

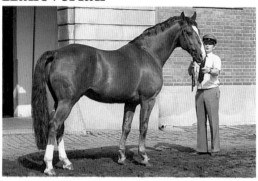

Character: Strong, sensible, versatile and willing.

History and origin: The development of this great German war horse was influenced by Britain's Hanoverian kings who, from the time of George I up until 1837 sent Thoroughbreds to Lower Saxony to improve the breed. However by the middle of the 18th century two distinct types had been developed, a lighter type for riding, and a heavier version for harness work. The most famous line was the Adeptus which descended from the Darley Arabian and, likewise, the Flick which descended from the Godolphin Arabian. Until 1914 nearly 60% of all Hanoverians came from one of these families.

Looks: Most solid horse colours. Two types, as aforesaid, both of strong bone and good quality.

Size: 15.3hh—17hh.

Uses: Driving, riding, competition.

Observations: Formerly a great war horse.

Pros and Cons: One of the best known breeds in Europe.

Hesse (Hessen)

Character: Strong, intelligent and versatile.

History and origin: This fine German horse which is bred at the State Stud of Dilenburg is yet another breed which is being developed to meet the needs of a geographical area. It is, however, based on its fellow-countryman, the Hanoverian.

Looks: Most solid horse colours.

Size: Approximately 15.3hh—17hh.

Uses: Driving, riding, competition work.

Observations: A regional variety based on Germany's most famous breed.

Pros and Cons: If you are a fan of the Hanoverian you are bound to favour the Hessen also.

Highland Pony

Character: Affectionate. Docile.

History and origin: The Highland pony has inhabited the Highlands of Scotland for many centuries. Most probably it is descended from ponies which migrated westwards from Northern Asia after the European Ice Age. Arabian blood has been introduced.

Looks: Bay, black, brown, chestnut and dun — there is often a stripe down the back — also, liver-chestnut with silver mane and tail. Small head, broad withers, short back and short, sturdy legs.

Size: 13.2hh—14.2hh. But there are smaller ponies. Indeed sometimes they are divided into three groups.

Uses: Extremely versatile. This is the mount famed for carrying stalkers in the Highlands, and as pack ponies. Indeed they are often associated with the British Queen Victoria, at Balmoral Castle. Nowadays, used mainly for pony trekking, driving and general pleasure riding.

Observations: Tough. Can be kept at grass all year round.

Pros and Cons: A strong, good natured animal that makes a good choice of youngster's riding and/or show pony.

Hispano (Spanish) Anglo Arab

Character: Courageous, intelligent, strong and lively.

History and origin: Spain's answer to the Anglo Arab was devised by crossings of Spanish Arab mares and English Thoroughbred stallions in the provinces of Estremadura and Andalucia resulting in an extremely stylish Anglo Arabian.

Looks: Colours are bay, chestnut and grey. Light and elegantly built with strong bone, long slender limbs and good feet.

Size: 15.1hh—16hh.

Uses: Army horse, eventing, competition and saddle horse.

Observations: Brave horse often used in its native land to test the spirit of young bulls destined for the Corrida (bullfight).

Pros and Cons: An obedient, versatile horse that often tends to resemble either the Arab or the Thoroughbred.

Holstein

Character: Docile and willing. Of great power and stamina.

History and origin: This is one of Germany's oldest breeds. It comes from Schleswig-Holstein in the west of Germany and dates back to the 14th century and a stable belonging to the monastery of Ueterson in a marshy area on the right bank of the Elbe estuary.

Looks: Colours are bay, brown, black, grey and chestnut. Straight back, sometimes quite long; well pronounced withers. Head and neck long; strong, well muscled legs. Longish ears and tail well set on and elegantly carried.

Size: 16.1hh—16.2hh.

Uses: Saddle horse, jumping, carriage and competition horse.

Observations: Former heavy war horse and later a gun horse used for pulling artillery. A number of breeds have contributed to the modern Holstein including the English Thoroughbred and Cleveland Bay. Neapolitan, Spanish and Oriental blood has also been added as has that of the Trakehner.

Pros and Cons: The Holstein has emerged as a first class jumper and eventer with a free flowing action.

Hunter

Character: Brave, sound and tireless.

History and origin: A Hunter is not a breed but a type, the type in fact that is best suited for the terrain over which it is to be used. The Thoroughbred is considered the ideal for the English Shires and much of the United States, but shorter legged, stronger animals are used in denser country. The warranty for a good hunter in the United Kingdom implies that the animal is sound in wind and eyes and is capable of being hunted.

Looks: Any horse colour. Good legs and a generous body which allows the heart, lungs and other organs to perform their function to the limit.

Size: This varies in different countries of the world. In the United Kingdom there are three classes of show hunter: *Lightweight:* 13 st and under. *Middleweight:* over 13 st and not exceeding 14st 7lbs. *Heavyweight:* over 14st 7lbs.

Uses: The value of a hunter has been described as being dependent on its ability to perform in a way required of a good hunter following hounds.

Observations: What is needed is a paragon of virtue with nerves of steel, soundness and stamina.

Pros and Cons: While the Thoroughbred is considered the ideal, many Cobs and children's ponies make splendid hunters.

Iceland (Icelandic Pony)

Character: Affectionate, docile and hardy.

History and origin: The Iceland is of mixed origin tracing back to the 9th century when Norwegian migrants brought their ponies to Iceland, the Norwegians in turn being joined by settlers from the Western Isles of Scotland who brought ponies of Celtic stock with them.

Looks: Colours are predominantly grey, but sometimes dun. Short, stocky body with large head, short, thick neck, expressive, intelligent eyes, heavy mane and forelock.

Size: 12hh—13hh.

Uses: Riding and pack pony. Also used for trekking.

Observations: There are two types: riding and draught. (Former Pit Pony working in the English coal mines).

Pros and Cons: A pony that can find its own way home and is controlled as much — if not more — by the voice than the aids.

Irish Draught

Character: Docile, intelligent and hard-working.

History and origin: Indigenous to Ireland and, in particular, Connemara, the Irish draught may originally have had a sprinkling of Arab and Spanish blood. However the first account of any crossing refers to the infusion of Thoroughbred blood in the 18th and early 19th centuries.

Looks: Colours are bay, brown, grey and chestnut. Well proportioned head, straight profile, long, straight back, prominent withers. Solid, muscular legs with a little feathering.

Size: 15hh—17hh.

Uses: Draught work. Agriculture. Riding.

Observations: Good jumper.

Pros and Cons: The Irish draught hunter is a national pride and the Government takes great pains to restrict the export of breed members.

Italian Heavy Draught

Character: Active, willing, good natured ... and fast.

History and origin: Traces back to 1860 when a stud farm at Ferrara in Italy commenced breeding stallions from the Po delta, later adding English Thoroughbred, Hackney and Oriental blood.

Later in an effort to produce a heavier animal, Ardennais, Boulonnais and Norfolk-Breton stallions were used also.

Looks: Colour is usually liver chestnut with flaxen mane and tail, but may be chestnut or roan.

Fairly long, elegant head, short, straight back, broad deep body and short legs with some feathering.

Size: 15hh—17hh.

Uses: Farm horse.

Observations: Very fast for such a large horse.

Pros and Cons: Mechanisation has caused numbers to decline. Many brood mares are, alas, kept for meat.

Jutland

Character: Excellent temperament. Docile and energetic.

History and origin: Comes from Jutland where it is still the most popular breed the origins of which trace back to the horse used by the Vikings.

In the 19th century it benefited from an infusion of Suffolk Punch and Cleveland Bay blood and, more recently, by that of the Ardennais.

Looks: Colours are usually chestnut with silver mane and tail, but may also be brown, bay, roan black and grey.

Well proportioned head with small eyes; short, arched neck; short, strong back, deep chest, short and strong muscular legs.

Size: 15.2hh—16hh.

Uses: Agricultural work, heavy draught.

Observations: Used as a charger in the Middle Ages.

Pros and Cons: A gentle giant bearing a strong similarity to the Schleswig, a breed bred in the western part of the Schleswig province in Prussia, once part of Denmark.

Karabair

Character: Agile, steady and good natured.

History and origin: The Karabair is an ancient breed of Mongol and Arab blood which is bred in the mountains of Uzbekistan in Central Asia.

Looks: Colours are usually chestnut, bay and grey, but may be other horse colours. It is a small thickset horse of good conformation, short, strong legs and sparse mane and tail.

Size: 14.2hh—15hh.

Uses: Tribesman's riding horse.

Observations: Used in the game of Kokpar (goat snatching) wherein a rider carries a goat which others, at full gallop, try to retrieve (or snatch) from him. This calls for incredible riding skill and agility on the part of the horse.

Pros and Cons: Hardy, light horse of speed and agility.

Konik

Character: Tough, powerful, good tempered and speedy.

History and origin: The word Konik is Polish for 'little horse', and there are several such animals bearing names such as Hucul, Zmudzin and Bilgoraj. The Bilgoraj Konik is believed to be a direct descendant of the wild horse.

Looks: Colours are normally mousey grey or dun with black dorsal stripe, also transverse stripes on forearms and second thighs. Well proportioned with rectangular shaped head.

Size: 11hh—14hh.

(The middle sized specimens are known as Mierzyn which means between two sizes.)

Uses: Children's ponies, draught work.

Observations: The Konik's ancestors lived wild in the forest of Bialowieza in Poland. They still roam free in the experimental stud of the Polish Academy of Science at Popeino, Mazury and other venues.

Pros and Cons: Pony of considerable endurance able to exist on poor feed and in severe climatic conditions.

Kisber

Character: Light, useful and competitive.

History and origin: One of a number of Hungarian half-breds, others being the Furioso, Gidran and Mezohegyes, the Kisber was developed at the Kisber Military Stud.

It is known that Holstein and Mecklenburg blood was used during the 19th century but it was the thoroughbred that contributed to its success as an event horse.

Looks: Any recognised solid horse colour. (See also the **Furioso**.)

Size: 15.1hh—16.2hh.

Uses: Lightweight sports and harness horse.

Observations: Docile and of great tractability.

Pros and Cons: Hungarian half-breds were used for military purposes in the days of the old Austrian Empire.

Kladruber

Character: Strong, elegant, gentle.

History and origin: Named after the Imperial Stud in Bohemia where it was bred and which is reputed to be the oldest operational stud in the world, the Kladruber derives from Spanish horses which found their way to both Austria and Bohemia from Spain and Italy.

Looks: Colours are grey or black. Roman nose, heavy crested neck; long, shallow body and round, muscular hindquarters.

Size: up to 17hh—18hh.

Uses: Was a State Carriage Horse. Still used for driving, but also as a riding horse.

Observations: Was used in teams of 6 or 8 or uniform colour on state occasions.

Pros and Cons: Noble beast, similar to, but heavier and taller than the Lipizzaner.

Knabstrup

Character: Gentle, strong, versatile.

History and origin: Ancient Danish breed of
spotted horse tracing back to the Napoleonic wars
when, in about 1808, Spanish military based in
Denmark left behind a spotted mare,
Flaebehoppen, of exceptional speed and endurance, which became the foundation mare of the
breed.

Looks: Appaloosa patterns on roan base (see
Appaloosa). Some variations in conformation.

Size: 15.1hh—16hh.

Uses: Circus, exhibition and riding horse.

Observations: There are a number of stud farms in
Denmark specialising in this attractive breed.

Pros and Cons: See comments on the **Appaloosa**.

Lipizzaner

Character: Graceful, gentle, dignified, intelligent and extremely versatile.

History and origin: The famous White Stallions of Vienna were founded as a breed in about 1580 by the Archduke Charles, son of the Emperor Ferdinand of Austria, who introduced Spanish, Italian and Arabian horses to produce a high class parade horse at Piber. The name Lipizzaner is taken from the location of the stud farm at Lipizza.

Looks: Colour may be any horse colour, but only grey stallions are used in the famous Spanish Riding School in Vienna. Long body, short legs, intelligent eyes, heavily crested neck.

Size: 15hh—16hh.

Uses: Famed for high school work, but also makes a fine riding and harness horse.

Observations: The famous dancing horses are born black, their coat lightening as they mature.

Pros and Cons: A joy to behold. Arguably the most beautiful and intelligent horses in the world about which a film and many books have been produced.

Lithuanian Heavy Draught

Character: Strong horse of considerable endurance.

History and origin: Recognised as a breed in 1963, this heavy horse is based mainly on the Zemaituke and imported Swedish Ardennes. The Zemaituka is an ancient breed indigenous to the grasslands of western Lithuania, one of the Baltic states.

Looks: Colours are predominantly bay, chestnut and grey. Deep chest, sturdy legs.

Size: Stallions: 16.2hh.
Mares: 15.3hh.

Uses: Agriculture, transport and, alas, let it be said, meat. Indeed they are crossed with other varieties to make them heavier - and meatier.

Observations: Has inherited much of the Zemaituka's powers of endurance and staying power.

Pros and Cons: Lively and athletic despite its sturdy build.

Lokai

Character: Agile, docile and speedy.

History and origin: Like the Karabair the Lokai is a heavy harness horse of mixed Arabian and Mongol blood. It has also been crossed with the Akhal Teke to improve stature. It comes from Uzbekistan in Central Asia and is a favourite with tribesmen.

Looks: Colours are bay, grey, chestnut and black — sometimes dun, occasionally with a gold sheen on the coat. Of light frame and deep body. Straight face, muscular neck, hard, strong feet.

Size: 13.3hh—14.3hh.

Uses: Sure footed mountain pony, either ridden or used as pack pony. Like the Karabair it is famed for participation in the game of Kopar, or goat snatching.

Observations: Has an amazing turn of speed.

Pros and Cons: Gentle and talented.

Note: Light saddle and pack horse bred in the mountains of Uzbekistan, and a heavier harness type in the valleys.

Lusitano

Character: Docile, brave and athletic.

History and origin: The Lusitano's ancestry is similar to that of the Andalucian. However it is widely believed that a number of brood mares found their way to Austria from their native Portugal where they were used as foundation stock for the Lipizzaner.

Looks: Usually grey. Good conformation. Small head with straight profile, small ears and expressive eyes. Short, rather thick neck; short, straight back, muscular legs.

Size: 16hh.

Uses: Light farm work. Famed for its traditional role as a bullfighter's horse 'rejoneador' facing the bull while mounted, a task which calls for considerable skill on the part of both horse and rider.

Observations: Can exist on poor keep and is easy to train and handle.

Pros and Cons: Famed in its native land. However numbers are diminishing along with the decline of horse drawn carriages with which they were once much associated.

Marbach
(Baden Württemburg)

Character: Athletic, docile, reliable and versatile.

History and origin: German warmbloods are, with the exception of the Trakehner, named after the region from which they originate, the Marbach or Baden-Württemburg being centred on the Marbach Stud, which was established in 1573 and today produces both coldbloods and the more athletic types of horse, the Baden Württemburg being based on the Trakehner. It has, however, a rich variety of crossbreeding in its veins, including Norman and Anglo Norman. The stud book goes back to 1895.

Looks: Most solid horse colours. Solidly built with freedom of movement. A regional variety of the original all purpose cob type Württemburg.

Size: 15.3hh—16.2hh.

Uses: Riding horse, light draught, agriculture.

Observations: Useful, general purpose cob.

Pros and Cons: A refined version of a Cob type carefully achieved through crossbreeding.

Morgan

Character: Docile and kind but lively. Chosen by the US Cavalry as its official remount horse - following exhaustive tests with other breeds - because of its strength, stamina and tractability.

History and origin: Named after Justin Morgan, a singing teacher from Vermont, USA, who, in the 1790s, accepted a small, bay stallion in part payment for a debt. Morgan discovered that the stallion (possibly of Arabian or Thoroughbred ancestry) had the ability to perpetrate its characteristics to an amazing degree and mares were sent to him from far and wide.

The Morgan is the official symbol of Vermont.

Looks: Colour is usually bay, but sometimes chestnut or black, often with white markings.

Size: 14.1hh—16.2hh.

Uses: Versatile, family horse, ideal for dressage, driving, pleasure riding or working cattle.

Observations: Robust. A good doer.

Pros and Cons: Smart, energetic kindly horse.

Murakoz

Character: Docile and lively.

History and origin: Originally from land adjoining the Mura river in Hungary, and developed through crossing local mares with Ardennes, Percheron and Noriker stallions, also with native Hungarian stock.

Looks: Colours are bay, brown, black, chestnut (mane, tail and leg feathering flaxen), grey. Fairly long, heavy head, short muscular neck, short back, low, broad withers, short, well developed legs.

Size: Approximately 16hh.

Uses: Farm work.

Observations: There are two distinct types, one being taller and heavier than its shorter, lighter fellow.

Pros and Cons: Numbers are, alas, dwindling.

Mustang (Mustang Bronco)

Character: Rebellious. The word 'Bronco' translated from the Spanish means rough, coarse and/or hard.

History and origin: A likely descendant of horses brought to the New World by Cortez (from Cuba) in 1519, the Mustang (mestengo - stranger (Sp)) was of Spanish, Arabian and Barb blood. Scrawny and lacking in quality, once broken it developed into a useful saddle horse, in fact the original 'cow pony'!

However the true Mustang has been overtaken by the range horse via the introduction of Arab, Thoroughbred, Standardbred and Morgan blood.

Looks: Colours are varied. Dun and Palomino predominate. Small and sturdy with strong feet, and a head reminiscent of the Barb. Could never be described as a beauty.

Size: 14.2hh—15.2hh.

Uses: Cattle cutting and range horse. Rodeo (bronco-busting) favourite.

Observations: Hardy. Cast-iron constitution.

Pros and Cons: Uncertain temperament. Courage. A decided pioneer of the old Wild West.

New Forest Pony

Character: Hardy, good natured family pony. Sound, sure footed. Much in demand by youngsters for Pony Club events.

History and origin: The New Forest Pony has run in the New Forest area in Hampshire, England, for about 1,000 years. The ponies are mentioned in Canute's Forest Law proclaimed at Winchester in 1016. However the New Forest Pony Breeding and Cattle Society was not set up until 1891.

Looks: These ponies were subjected to many outcrosses: Arab, Thoroughbred, Welsh, Dartmoor, Exmoor, Highfield and Fell. There was no definite type and there is still far more variation in size and colour than in any other British pony breeds. Any colour except piebald and skewbald is acceptable.

Size: 12hh—14.2hh with a good sloping shoulder.

Uses: General purpose family pony.

Observations: A tough, native pony that may be stabled or kept at grass.

Pros and cons: Ideal child's mount.

Nonius

Character: Gentle, quiet and willing.

History and origin: Hungarian breed named after its founder, an Anglo-Norman stallion of that name, out of a Norman mare and an English half bred stallion captured by the Austrians following their victory over Napoleon at the battle of Leipzig. Nonius thereafter sired some excellent progeny at the Mezohegyes Stud in Hungary. He was put to Andalucian, Arab, Kladruber, English half-breds, Lipizzaner and Norman mares.

Looks: Colours are usually black or brown. Attractive, longish head, long, muscular neck, broad back, sloping shoulders, muscular quarters, solid limbs.

Size: Large Nonius about 17hh.
Small Nonius about 15hh (two types).

Uses: Riding horse and/or light draught work, according to type.

Observations: Does not usually mature until about 6 years of age, but is very long lived.

Pros and Cons: Pleasant horse with excellent action. Not all that hardy, so make sure you have a stable.

Noric - Noriker

Character: Adaptable, willing, sure-footed.

History and origin: Small cart horse of ancient origin named after the Roman province of Noricum (which at that time entailed much of modern Austria). Possibly had its roots in Northern Greece from which venue the Romans obtained local stock.

Looks: Colours are bay, black, dun, chestnut and grey. Also, very occasionally, spotted. Large common head, thick neck, broad chest, short legs with some feathering.

Size: 16hh—16.2hh.

Uses: Agriculture. Mountain work.

Observations: There are two types, the Oberlander and the spotted Pinzgauer.

Pros and Cons: Popular in its native land. Little seen elsewhere.

Norman Cob

Character: It is, or should be, a 'perfect gentleman'.

History and origin: Developed at the beginning of the 19th century. This was the time when a different type of mount was required for riding to that destined for agricultural work. The work horses were bred along similar lines to those in the United Kingdom (see the **Cob**).

Looks: Colours are generally bay, black, brown, chestnut or grey. The Cob has a short back and great girth. Its quality head is set on a neck which is arched and elegant. The tail is carried high with gaiety. The mane is hogged.

Size: No more than 15.3hh.

Uses: Hacking, hunting, agriculture.

Observations: Up to weight.

Pros and Cons: The Cob is built for comfort - and reliability.

North Swedish

Character: Energetic, tough and willing. Takes life in its stride.

History and origin: Traces back to the ancient native Scandinavian horse and, since 1890, has been crossed only with the Døle (Døle Gudbrandsdal). A stud book was established in 1924.

Looks: Colours are bay, black, brown, chestnut and dun. Medium sized, deep bodied, fairly heavy head, long ears, shortish legs with good bone and feathering behind fetlock.

Size: Mares 15.1hh.
Stallions 15.2hh.

Uses: Army. Agriculture.

Observations: The North Swedish Trotter is a light strain of the North Swedish and is bred specially for this purpose.

Pros and Cons: Long lived, speedy for size and remarkably disease resistant.

Oldenberg

Character: Calm, brave, willing.

History and origin: Traces back to the Friesian with introduction of Spanish, Anglo-Arab, English Thoroughbred and Neapolitan stallion blood. Cleveland Bay contributed towards the end of the 19th century.

Found fame via Count Anton Gunther (1603-1667) owner of the fine Oldenberg stallion, Kranich.

Looks: Colours are bay, black, brown, chestnut and grey. Heavy head and neck. Flat ribs, sloping shoulders, muscular legs.

Size: 16.2hh—17.2hh.

Uses: Riding, light draught, jumping.

Observations: Matures early. Not renowned for endurance or toughness.

Pros and Cons: The heaviest of the German warmblood horses, it retains many coldblood characteristics.

Note: There is a lighter version bred in Bavaria which always has a chestnut coat.

Orlov Trotter

Character: Gentle with plenty of stamina.

History and origin: Originated in 1777 by Count Alexis Gregorievich Orlov who developed the breed through crossing Arab, English Thoroughbred, Danish, Dutch and Mecklenburg breeds. The foundation stallion was an Arab, 'Smetanka', which was put to a Dutch mare.

Looks: There are two types, the heavier of which is generally black in colour, the lighter grey with pronounced Arab characteristics.

Fine looking horse with small Arab head, broad chest, long back, strong, muscular legs and good quarters.

Size: Up to 17hh.

Uses: Trotting races. Improvement of breeding stock.

Observations: Once the most renowned trotter in the world, it was overtaken by the American Standardbred following the Russian Revolution when breeding was interrupted.

Pros and Cons: A strong and elegant horse that can also be used for driving.

Paint Horse (Pinto)

Character: Docile, good beginner's horse.

History and origin: The Pinto (Paint horse) has been recognised since 1963 by the American Paint Horse Association. While, as stated elsewhere (see the **Pinto**) this is more of a colour than a breed, two stallions, Sheik and Sun Cloud, are regarded as the founders of the type.

Looks: There are two eligible markings: the Tobiano with white legs, white over the withers and smooth patches of colour on neck, chest, flank and buttocks. The Overo has more solid colour with patches of white. Legs are usually coloured.

Size: 14.3hh—15.3hh.

Uses: Famed as Indian war horse, but makes good polo pony, hunter and jumper. Excellent in riding schools.

Observations: Good doer. Tough.

Pros and Cons: Fine novice choice, but very noticeable.

Palomino

Isabella - Golden horse of the West

Character: Generally docile and affectionate.

History and origin: Such horses, of Spanish origin, with Arab and Barb blood, were firm favourites of Queen Isabella of Spain, and became known as Isabellas in her honour. Controversy exists as to whether the type found its way to the New World with Columbus, who was sponsored by Queen Isabella, or with Cortez, who had them with him in Mexico in 1519. At any rate, it was Cortez who presented one of these mounts to Count Juan de Palomino whose name has become synonymous with the variety.

Looks: Colour should be that of a gold coin, with light mane and tail. Similar to the Arab or Barb but more solidly built.

Uses: Good saddle horse, cow pony, show jumper and general pleasure riding horse.

Observations: In truth more a colour than a breed.

Pros and Cons: The smaller version is a great favourite with youngsters, particularly in the United Kingdom for Pony Club events.

Percheron

Character: Affectionate, gentle and easy to handle.

History and origin: Originated about one hundred years ago in the La Perche district of France and generally believed to have derived from the powerful, short legged work horse of Belgium and Northern France.

Looks: Colours are black and grey only, sometimes with a very little white. Short, compact body of tremendous depth. Head wide across eyes which should be full and docile. Great bone, but in spite of size and weight extremely active and agile. Good hard blue feet, legs as clean as possible.

Size: Stallions not less than 16.3hh.
Mares not less than 16hh.

Uses: A heavy draught horse claimed to be the most economical of its kind.

Observations: Popular throughout the world. Probably the most widely dispersed horse of its kind.

Pros and Cons: Admirable heavy horse in every way.

Pinto (Painted Horse)

Character: Docile, good beginner's horse.

History and origin: Paint horse/Painted horse/Pinto — USA; Piebald (black and white); Skewbald (brown and white) UK.

Looks: More a colour than a breed though a Pinto Horse Society and an American Paint Horse Association have been formed in the USA. Most likely developed by the American Indians as a means of camouflage.

Size: 14.3hh—15.3hh.

Uses: Famed as an Indian war horse, but works in harness and is a popular first mount and riding school horse. Also the traditional Gypsy's horse and trade cart pony.

Observations: Good doer. Tough.

Pros and Cons: Excellent choice for the novice rider who doesn't mind standing out in the crowd.

Pony of the Americas

Character: Docile. Easy to handle.

History and origin: A relatively new breed (1956), which is a blend of Appaloosa, Arabian and Quarter horse. The progenitor, 'Black Hand', was foaled out of an Appaloosa mare which had been mated with a Shetland stallion.

Looks: Coat patterns like those of the Appaloosa, including the sclera and, occasionally, striped hooves.

Size: 11.2hh—13.2hh.

Uses: A good jumper and used for both trekking and long distance riding.

Observations: Hardy, with considerable powers of endurance.

Pros and Cons: A useful and attractive mount much favoured by young riders.

Przevalski (Wild Horse)

Character: Strong, energetic and courageous.

History and origin: The skin and skull of a Przevalski or Asiatic or Mongolian wild horse, was discovered in 1881 by a Russian explorer. Professor M. Przevalski, in whose honour the name *Equus Przevalski* was bestowed on the horse. Considered to be the ancestor of all breeds of horses and ponies, the Przevalski has, since living memory, inhabited a specific area in Northern Sinkiang in Mongolia.

Looks: Colour is dun with a mealy muzzle, often a faint black or brown stripe on the back and a little black beneath knees and hocks. Described by Lydekker in *The Horse and its Relations* as being 'intermediate in character between the horse on the one hand and the kiang and onager on the other, having chestnuts on all four limbs, compact build, strong limbs'.

Size: 12.2hh—14.2hh.

Uses: Lives wild. Largest herd is at Prague. Also distributed throughout zoos, including Marwell, Hampshire and Whipsnade, Bedfordshire, in England.

Observations: Seems to have changed little since the last Ice Age. May once have been ridden by the Chinese.

Pros and Cons: Doesn't care for other horse breeds, preferring to be with its own kind.

Quarter Horse (American)

Character: Combines good disposition with keen intelligence. Gentle enough to be entrusted with children's safety, but with plenty of 'get up and go'.

History and origin: Developed by Colonial settlers at the beginning of the 17th century. Racing enthusiasts found that a cross between the English Blood horse (Thoroughbred) and the Indian (Chickasaw) pony, produced an animal with an incredible burst of speed over a short distance. Races were usually no more than a quarter of a mile, hence the name, officially selected by the American Quarter Horse Association at its inception in 1940.

Looks: Colours vary from black and chestnut to dun, grey and Palomino. Sturdy, powerfully built horse with very well developed hind quarters. Alert intelligence reflected by short, broad head topped by little 'foxy' ears, wide set, kind eyes, sensitive nostrils, short muzzle and firm mouth.

Size: 14.1hh—16hh.

Uses: Adaptable to just about any form of equine activity.

Observations: Easy to keep, thrifty and robust.

Pros and Cons: Ideal, versatile 'Friend of the Family'. Easy to train. Fast.

Rheinish Warmblood

Character: Powerful and willing.

History and origin: The Rhineland Heavy Draught (Rheinish German Coldblood) was a massive horse bred in Western Germany and the Brabant. Numbers diminished along with their agricultural use and the Rheinish Stud Book began to concentrate on registering warmbloods using the blood of Arabs, Russian saddle horses, the Don, Russian Trotter, the Akhal Teke and English Thoroughbred.

Looks: Colours are usually sorrel, brown or roan, but may be other horse colours. Long, arched neck, good general conformation.

Size: Up to 16.2hh but variable.

Uses: Versatile riding horse. Good trotter.

Observations: The Warmblood of today bears little resemblance to the heavy draught type of yesteryear but has inherited its strength and stamina.

Pros and Cons: Now also used for dressage and hunting, this breed, like others in Germany, has been designed to meet the needs of specific areas.

Russian Heavy Draught

Character: Docile and willing.

History and origin: Evolved over the last 100 years or so from local cart horse mares crossed with heavy draught horses, for example, the Belgian heavy draught, Swedish Ardennes, the Percheron and, indeed, the Orlov Trotter. It was specifically produced to meet the needs of the farming community in the Ukraine.

Looks: Colours are usually bay, chestnut or roan. Small and compact with medium sized head and short, thick neck. Strong hindquarters, legs have little feathering. Long tail and flowing mane.

Size: Approximately 14.2hh.

Uses: Heavy draught. Agriculture.

Observations: Used to be known as the Russian Ardennes.

Pros and Cons: Strong and hardy with pleasing appearance.

Russian Trotter

Character: Keen, intelligent and graceful.

History and origin: The Russians having reigned supreme in harness racing until the end of the 19th century with the Orlov Trotter, found themselves overtaken by the speedier American Standardbred. Later these American horses were imported and crossed with the Orlov. From such select crossings the Russian Trotter emerged and was recognised in 1949.

Looks: Colour is generally bay but may be black, chestnut or grey. Straight face, deep body, muscular back, fine, hard legs. Good general conformation.

Size: 15.3hh—16hh.

Uses: Harness racing.

Observations: There have been infusions of American blood over the years.

Pros and Cons: A specific result of the crossing of the Orlov Trotter and the American Standardbred.

Salerno

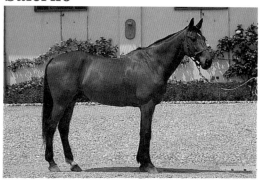

Character: Docile, keen.

History and origin: Descendant of the Neapolitan which was popular in the middle ages and bestowed with frequent infusions of Oriental and Spanish blood. Traces back to the rule of Charles II, King of Naples - later of Spain - who promoted this horse from 1763.

Looks: Colours are bay, black, chestnut and grey. Straight profile, fairly pronounced muscular withers, deep girth, good conformation and stance.

Size: 16.1hh—17hh.

Uses: Riding horse. Jumping.

Observations: Noted for its staying power.

Pros and Cons: English Thoroughbred blood having replaced that of the Arab, the customary grey is now rare.

Schleswig

Character: Docile, strong and willing.

History and origin: Heavy draught type bred in the plentiful grazing land found in Schleswig province. Traces back to the Jutland horse of Denmark and was similarly endowed with Suffolk Punch blood via the stallion, Oppenhein LXII.

Looks: Colours are bay, chestnut, grey (usually with white markings), slightly convex profile, short, muscular neck, strong back, deep chest, fairly short, muscular legs.

Size: 15.2hh—16hh.

Uses: Artillery horse. Agriculture.

Observations: Carried armoured knights in the Middle Ages.

Pros and Cons: Schleswig province was at one time Danish, and a glimpse of the heavy Danish horse is still occasionally to be seen.

Shagya (Hungarian Shagya)

Character: Athletic, hardy and versatile.

History and origin: Hungarian breed derived from a desert bred Arabian stallion from which its name comes. The foundation stallion, Shagya, was foaled in 1830 and brought by the Bedouins to stand at stud at Babolna in Hungary.

Looks: Usually grey. Most of the qualities of the Arab.

Size: 14hh—15hh.

Uses: Athletic sports and general riding horse.

Observations: Can survive on poor keep.

Pros and Cons: Beautiful breed that is somewhat tougher than the Arab.

Shetland Pony

Character: Perky. Lovable.

History and origin: The smallest native British breed which has, for centuries, inhabited the Shetland Islands of Scotland. Its remains on these Islands date back to the Bronze Age. However it did not reach the mainland until the 19th century.

Looks: Colours: black, bay, brown, chestnut or parti-coloured. Head broad, fairly straight face, large, kind eyes, small muzzle with pronounced nostrils, short ears, straight back, plentiful mane and tail.

Size: Not more than 10.2hh.

Uses: Originally used mainly as a pack pony carrying peat for the Islanders' fires. Later it was used extensively as a pit pony in the mines. Nowadays kept almost solely as a child's riding pony and/or pet.

Observations: Tough. Can be kept at grass all year round. Long lived.

Pros and Cons: Superb child's first mount and/or child's (or adult's) pet. But remember that it is very strong for its size and can be wilful.

Shire

Character: Gentle and willing.

History and origin: England's greatest agricultural horse, believed to be a descendant of the Great Horse of mediaeval times which carried riders in armour. Although generally thought of as a British breed it was originally created in the Netherlands by crossings of the largest and strongest draught horses in Europe.

Looks: Colours are usually bay and brown, but may also be black or grey. Often have much white on feet and legs, with ample feathering. Lean head, broad forehead, long, muscular neck, short back, broad muscular chest with rounded ribs. Fairly short legs.

Size: Over 17hh.

Uses: Heavy draught. Agriculture.

Observations: Considerable strength and stamina allied to docility.

Pros and Cons: Revival of interest is resulting in export to many countries of the world.

Skewbald

Character: Docile. Good beginner's horse.

History and origin: More a colour than a breed. Both Skewbalds and Piebalds (black and white) are known as Pintos in America.

Looks: A horse or pony is skewbald where its skin bears large, irregular patches of white hair and any definite colour (usually brown) except black.

Size: Up to 15.3hh.

Uses: Famed as an Indian horse, but works in harness and is a popular first mount and riding school horse. Also the traditional Gypsy's pony and trade cart animal.

Observations: Good doer. Tough.

Pros and Cons: Useful horse that is often under-rated.

Skyros

Character: Quiet. Dependable.

History and origin: Ancient breed which takes its name from the Aegean island of Skyros where it has been used for farm work for many centuries. It is said to bear some resemblance to the Tarpan which was the original primitive wild horse of Europe (see **Przevalski**).

Looks: Colours are bay, brown, dun and grey. Small head, straight profile, short, thick neck, short back, slender legs.

Size: 9.2hh—11hh.

Uses: Local agriculture and pack pony. Makes good children's riding pony when exported.

Observations: No beauty because of poor shoulders and cow hocks.

Pros and Cons: Has much to commend it as a child's mount if properly reared and looked after.

American Standardbred

Character: Brave and willing with placid nature and great stamina.

History and origin: Renowned American pacing and trotting horse, the father of which is recorded under the name and number of 'Hambletonian 10' in the stud registry.

'Hambletonian 10' was a descendant of the English Thoroughbred, 'Messenger' which was imported into the USA in 1788 where it stood at stud founding a dynasty of trotters.

Looks: Usually bay, black, brown and chestnut (grey and roan are rare). Has thoroughbred looks, but is of stronger build, longer body and shorter legs.

Size: 15.2hh—16hh.

Uses: Mainly used competitively for harness racing.

Observations: More robust than the Thoroughbred and has greater powers of endurance.

Pros and Cons: Fast competitive horse that has also proved its worth in flat racing and in the hunting field.

Sorraia

Character: Tough, reliable, independent but biddable.

History and origin: Pony of ancient origin native to Western Spain and Portugal where it lives wild.

Looks: Colour is dun and grey often with Zebra markings on legs and a dorsal eel stripe. Some resemblance to the Tarpan and Przevalski (Asiatic wild horse). Large head, long, thin neck, straight back, poorly developed chest, long, sturdy legs.

Size: 12.2hh—13hh.

Uses: Makes good riding and pack pony when broken.

Observations: Becoming rare.

Pros and Cons: Regarded as Spain's only native pony. (In fact it inhabits the Spanish-Portuguese borders.)

Suffolk Punch

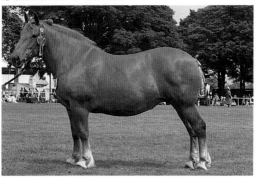

Character: Active and economical.

History and origin: Always referred to as the Suffolk Punch and, with the exception of the Percheron, the only clean-legged, heavy cart horse in England, the Suffolk Punch traces back in direct male line to a horse foaled in 1760. There have been occasional infusions of foreign blood which have resulted in a more refined forehead and greater vigour.

Looks: Colour is always chestnut. Large head, muscular quarters, great width in front and behind.

Size: About 16hh.

Uses: Agriculture. Has great pulling power. Also been used by the Army.

Observations: Described as 'round and impressive'.

Pros and Cons: Good natured and inexpensive to keep.

Swedish Warmblood

Character: Athletic, intelligent.

History and origin: Developed from native stock with infusions of Prussian, Hanoverian and Thoroughbred blood. Known since the 17th century.

Looks: Any solid horse colours. Well proportioned head, long, straight back, prominent withers, broad chest, deep girth, strong, well muscled legs.

Size: 16.2hh—17hh.

Uses: General purpose riding horse. Jumping, dressage.

Observations: Well proportioned and quiet with considerable stamina.

Pros and Cons: The fact that this horse is widely exported surely speaks for itself.

Tennessee Walking Horse

Plantation Walking Horse

Character: Docile. Easy to handle.

History and origin: The foundation stallion is credited as 'Black Allan', a Standardbred (foaled 1886) of Morgan and Hambletonian ancestry. 'Black Allan' covered Tennessee mares of various pacing, saddle horse and Thoroughbred ancestry.

Traditionally the breed performs a flat-footed running walk with considerable over-reach of the hind hooves; also a canter. However it does trot and have other paces.

Looks: Colours are bay, black, brown, chestnut, grey and roan. More powerfully built, and less elegant, than the American Saddle horse, the Tennessee Walking horse is a larger, heavier animal with an arched, muscular neck, straight back, muscular legs and nicked tail, carried high.

Size: 15hh—16hh.

Uses: Developed for pleasure riding, driving and farm (plantation) work. Also a popular show horse.

Observations: Little seen outside the USA.

Pros and Cons: An extremely comfortable ride whose walk does not require any posting - rising to the trot. It is the ideal mount for novices, the elderly and/or those destined to spend many hours in the saddle.

Tersk (Tersky)

Character: Gentle and intelligent.

History and origin: The Tersk was developed in the 1920s in the Stavropol region of Russian. However its origins trace back to a now extinct breed, the Strelet, that was used by the Cossacks. The breed, which has also benefited from infusions of blood from the Arab, Don, English Thoroughbred and Kabardin, was officially recognised in 1948.

Looks: Colour is usually silvery grey, but may be bay or chestnut. Well proportioned head, straight back, prominent withers, well muscled legs.

Size: 14.3hh—15.1hh.

Uses: Extremely versatile. Dressage. Jumping, light draught, saddle horse. Circus performer.

Observations: Docile, intelligent and suited to a wide variety of tasks.

Pros and Cons: Worthwhile animal of considerable endurance.

Thoroughbred (English)

Character: Skittish and highly strung.

History and origin: The English Thoroughbred, arguably the fastest, most beautiful, and sought after horse in the world, traces its ancestry in the male line for 30 generations to three Arab stallions, which were imported into England about 300 years ago. These were the Byerley Turk, the Darley Arabian and the Godolphin Arabian. During the 17th century, English racing enthusiasts aimed to increase the speed of their horses by crossing home bred mares with imported Arab stallions. The then British king, Charles II, also imported Eastern mares, the blood of which was introduced to those mares which were in his stables, including some of Oriental blood which had come from Spain.

Looks: Colours are bay, black, chestnut, grey, roan and, very occasionally, red roan, often with white markings. Small, refined head, long, arched neck, pronounced withers, deep body, short back, clean, hard legs.

Size: 14.3hh—17hh (Average about 16hh).

Uses: Racing, eventing, dressage, competitive events, hunting.

Observations: The Thoroughbred Stud Book, in England, dates back to 1791.

Pros and Cons: Creature of beauty, speed and stamina.

Thoroughbred (French)

Character: Skittish and highly strung.

History and origin: (See the **English Thoroughbred**.) Over the years many countries of the world have imported English Thoroughbred stock and developed their own thoroughbred lines. The French Thoroughbred gained national official breed status in the 1830s and their horses now certainly give those of the British a 'run for their money'. Most French Thoroughbred breeding is carried out at studs in the areas around Paris and Normandy.

Looks: See **English Thoroughbred**.

Size: Average 16hh.

Uses: Racing, eventing, dressage, hunting.

Observations: The Grand Prix de Paris, an international thoroughbred race, was begun in 1863. Two years later a French horse, Gladiateur, won the British Triple Crown.

Pros and Cons: Good stayer.

Toric

Character: Gentle. Quiet to handle.

History and origin: The Toric has been developed over the past century. The Klepper, a draught horse derived from the Arab and the Ardennes has, in every case, played a part, but the blood of the English Thoroughbred, Orlov Trotter and the Trakehner were also added.

Looks: Colours are bay, dark bay, chestnut and grey, with white markings. Medium sized head with straight profile, long ears, low withers, slightly hollow back, short, solid legs and sloping shoulders.

Size: 15hh—15.2hh.

Uses: Agriculture. Light draught.

Observations: Because of its ancestry looks somewhat refined for a draught horse.

Pros and Cons: Ideal if you want a worker that looks like a great, heavy riding horse.

Trakehner (East Prussian)

Character: Good tempered. Easy on the eye. Hardy.

History and origin: The Trakehner stud, the Newmarket of Germany, was founded by Frederick William I of Prussia (father of Frederick the Great) in 1732. A number of different breeds were installed with a view to establishing a Royal Mews. While Oriental blood was contributed in the formation of the breed and, notably Arab stallions from Prince Radziwill's stud in Poland, the most important stallion was probably the Thoroughbred, 'Perfectionist' by 'Persimmom' out of 'Perfect Dream'.

Looks: Only solid horse colours, but light specimens are unusual. Regal head, long, crested neck, strong back of medium length and muscular quarters.

Size: 16hh—16.2hh.

Uses: Army military horse, hunting, general purpose. Competition.

Observations: Brave and elegant. Has been used to improve Hanoverian and other German breeds.

Pros and Cons: Excellent action and conformation.

Ukraine (Ukraine Riding Horse)

Character: Sound temperament.

History and origin: A saddle horse developed in Ukrainian studs following World War II by the crossing of German Hanoverians, Trakehners and English Thoroughbred stallions with breeds that included the Nonius, Gidran and Furioso North Star mares.

Looks: Colours are bay, black and chestnut. Largish head with straight profile, eyes have alert expression, high withers, long, sloping shoulders, strong legs.

Size: 15.3hh mares. 16.3hh stallions.

Uses: Sports horse, dressage, light draught.

Observations: Hindquarters may be under-developed but the horse is generally well muscled.

Pros and Cons: Has been developed in much the same manner as the English hunter.

Viatka

Character: Fast, strong and hardy.

History and origin: Developed in Viatka and in the northern Kazan provinces of Russian using the Estonian pony, the Klepper, with both Finnish and Oriental blood.

Looks: Colours are bay, dun, grey and roan (often with eel stripe and zebra markings on legs), black mane and tail; head tends to be heavy, short back, pronounced withers, sloping shoulders, strong legs.

Size: 13hh—14hh.

Uses: Agriculture. Light draught.

Observations: There are, in fact, two types, the Obvinka, which is the taller of the two and the Kazanka.

Pros and Cons: Very strong, well made pony.

Vladimir

Character: Gentle and willing.

History and origin: Developed at the turn of the
century in Vladimir, Russia, when local mares
were crossed with a number of heavy draught
breeds, among which were the Ardennais,
Clydesdale, Cleveland Bay, Percheron, Shire and
Suffolk Punch.

Following the Russian Revolution, the best
examples were bred in order to establish a fixed
type. Registration was achieved in 1946.

Looks: Colours are bay, brown, black, chestnut;
the black may have white markings. Powerful,
well proportioned, heavy draught horse of
medium size. Has a large head, Roman nose,
broad back and long, feathered limbs.

Size: 15.1hh—16hh.

Uses: Draught work. Also pulls local troika sleighs.

Observations: Selection is carried out by trial in
which the horse has to pull extremely heavy
loads.

Pros and Cons: Predominantly reared in the region
of Vladimir, and also Ivanovo where the breed
originated.

Welsh Cob

Character: Strong, kind, versatile.

History and origin: A likely descendant of the Welsh Mountain pony, but a larger animal the exact origins of which have been lost in the mists of antiquity.

Looks: Colours are bay, black, brown, dun, chestnut, grey and roan. Small head with prick ears. Very strong body with deep girth and powerful quarters; there is a little, fine hair upon the heels. Tail was customarily docked up until 1949 when the practice became illegal in the United Kingdom.

Size: 14hh—15.1hh.

Uses: Pleasure riding, harness work, hunting and jumping.

Observations: Strong, reliable horse. Comfortable.

Pros and Cons: Excellent family mount. Equally suited to a young rider or a somewhat portly, elderly gentleman who wishes to hack and/or hunt.

Welsh Mountain Pony

Character: Brave, intelligent, lively.

History and origin: Often described as one of the most beautiful of England's native ponies, the Welsh Mountain - not to be confused with the Welsh Pony - is a likely descendant of native stock crossed with imports from the Orient as long ago as 55BC.

Looks: Any known horse colour excepting piebald and skewbald. The Welsh Mountain pony has a short, sturdy body, short limbs, pronounced withers and a deep chest and girth. Its ears are pointed and it has an Arab-type head and large, very expressive eyes.

Size: Not over 12hh.

Uses: Show pony, pleasure riding, light draught, pony trekking.

Observations: Used extensively for pony trekking in the Black Mountain area of Wales. Exceedingly strong and sure footed for size. Well up to weight.

Pros and Cons: Excellent choice for the novice.

Welsh Pony

Character: Brave, docile, intelligent.

History and origin: Derived from Welsh Cob and Welsh Mountain pony stock, but with an infusion of Hackney blood. Its Arab head is owed to 'Merlin', a small English Thoroughbred stallion, which was a descendant of the Darley Arabian.

Looks: Any known horse colours excepting piebald and skewbald. Similar in appearance to the Welsh Mountain pony, but larger, with neat Arabian head and thoroughbred eyes.

Size: 12.2hh—13.2hh.

Uses: Children's pony, light draught.

Observations: Strong. Great powers of endurance. Can be kept at grass.

Pros and Cons: Agile. Energetic. Makes a great youngster's show pony.

Westphalian

Character: Athletic, intelligent.

History and origin: One of Germany's most popular breeds the Westphalian, like other German warmbloods, is not pure bred and the stud book is still open. Indeed the Hanoverian has played a large part in its development as one of the world's top competition horses.

Looks: Any solid horse colour. A heavy made version of the Hanoverian with strong quarters and good bone.

Size: 15.2hh—16.2hh.

Uses: Dressage, show jumping, driving, all round sports horse.

Observations: The breed association was established in 1826. Stallions at Warendorf State Stud undergo strict ability and temperament tests and receive a training score. Only those achieving a high score are permitted to stand at stud.

Pros and Cons: A breed that has gone for Gold - and got it - at the Olympics!

Wiekopolska

Character: Brave and well balanced.

History and origin: A comparatively new, Polish breed based on two other breeds, the Poznan and the Masuran, as well as several other horses, all of which had varying amounts of Arab, English Thoroughbred and East Prussian blood. Oriental and Trakehner/East Prussian stallions have all contributed.

Looks: Colours are bay, brown, black, chestnut and grey. Sturdy horse with long, straight back and slightly prominent withers, slightly arched neck and long, muscular legs.

Size: 15.1hh—16.1hh.

Uses: Riding and light draught.

Observations: A legacy of the Trakehner stud remaining after it was destroyed in World War II.

Pros and Cons: Gentle horse currently being developed for sports purposes at a number of Polish studs.

Würtemberg

Character: Gentle and well balanced.

History and origin: Developed at the Marbach Stud at the beginning of the 16th century by crossings of local mares with Arab, Oldenberg, Nonius, Norman, Anglo Norman and Trakehner blood.

Looks: Colours are bay, brown, black and chestnut with white markings. Square, average-sized head, long straight back, pronounced withers; strong, muscular legs.

Size: About 16hh.

Uses: Agriculture. Light draught. Riding horse.

Observations: The Stud Book traces back to 1895.

Pros and Cons: Well made horse that is hardy and good natured.

Choosing a Horse or Pony

Buying a horse or pony is not a step to be taken lightly. A beginner buying a skittish thoroughbred mount is tantamount to a Learner Driver taking possession of a high-powered sports car. Cost of feed and livery (stable hire) must be taken into consideration if the buyer is not one of the lucky few who own outbuildings and grazing land and, in every case, there is the added expense of the animal's tack, that is, its saddle, bridle, rugs and other equipment, not to mention regular shoeing and the inevitable veterinary bills that will arise.

Parents should not accede to a child's pleas for a pony in the mistaken belief that the animal can fend for itself in a field provided that it is watered and thrown the occasional bale of hay, any more than the child should be allowed to canter, even jump, a pony that has not done any work for months and which must slowly be brought back into condition if its heart is not to be adversely affected.

So where does one begin to find the right mount and how do we know that it is healthy?

Bearing in mind that the sturdy native pony or cob type is the best bet for the inexperienced or nervous rider rather than a spirited Arab or thoroughbred type which is more suited to the accomplished, competitive rider, horses and ponies are advertised in equine magazines such as, in the United Kingdom, the long-established and well-respected, *Horse and Hound*, and in the livestock columns of country newspapers. There are regular Horse and Pony Sales which are advertised in equine periodicals and there are dealers. Horses and ponies can sometimes be purchased from a riding stables where, for example, a client has perhaps been riding a favourite mount for some time and persuades the proprietor to part with it — or to look out for something similar.

There is much to be said for buying a child's pony in this way. It is likely to be quiet, well schooled and traffic proof though having been accustomed to going out on school rides it may need training to hack out without an equine companion.

Buying a horse or pony at auction is a chancy business unless you are accompanied by a knowledgeable judge of horse flesh — which is in all cases a sensible precaution. However, animals in the sale ring are generally sold with a warranty, which does afford some measure of protection.

Sometimes a private advertiser will allow a horse or pony to go out 'on trial'. But if this is the case they will most likely expect the proposed buyer to take out insurance lest any fate should befall the steed while in their care. Few buyers will embark on a purchase unless it is subject to veterinary inspection, and the obtaining of a certificate to the effect that the mount is, in the veterinarian's opinion, of an approximate age and suitable for light hacking and/or all general purposes as the case may be.

Finally a reminder for the novice that it is often possible to obtain a horse or pony from a rescue centre provided that they can satisfy the official that they will be a responsible owner and can provide the necessary facilities. And that an older mount is likely to prove more suitable for them than a frisky youngster.

Stable Equipment and Management

Book a riding lesson or hire a hack from a stables and, likely as not, the animal will be groomed until it gleams and tacked up (saddled and bridled) to await your pleasure.

Owning your own mount is a very different story involving many hours of hard work feeding, grooming, exercising, mucking out and tack-cleaning every single day of the year unless, that is, the horse is in what is known as full livery where again these tasks are done for you in return for an appropriate fee.

Riding schools offer lessons in equitation (riding). Livery stables (or yards) provide facilities for privately owned horses and ponies. The facilities range from full livery where the owner has nothing to do but present himself and tack up the mount, to part-livery, do-it-yourself livery and grass livery.

Part livery might, for example, involve the yard in providing the mount's stable and feed and mucking out leaving the owner to do the grooming and exercising or it might only involve mucking out and turn out, in other words turning the horse out for a couple of hours every day into a paddock or exercise ring. There are many variations of the part livery arrangement and these are usually worked out between the owner and the livery yard's proprietor.

Do-it-yourself livery, the most popular and less expensive, except for grass livery where a stable is not provided, means what it says, the owner rents a stable, generally what is known as a loose box, has the use of an area for feed and hay storage, communal tack room and shared grazing facilities, but the task of looking after the mount is theirs and theirs alone and they must be prepared to muck out their mount's bed which means cleaning out the animal's droppings and replacing its bedding with fresh straw or shavings.

Feeding

The horse kept at grass can graze at will. Because horses have small stomachs and need to eat little and often it is necessary for the stabled animal to have an adequate supply of hay. Both the stabled horse and that which is kept at grass must always have a fresh water supply.

In the same manner as a car needs petrol and oil if it is to perform efficiently, the horse's rations must be regulated according to the tasks it is being asked to undertake.

The horse in strenuous work will need at least 4.5kg - 5.4kg of hay every day, more like 6.8kg if it is being hunted broken down into regular feeds, for instance in early morning, noon, afternoon and evening. But let it be said that there are many busy owners who manage with just an early morning feed, before they go to their office, and another in the evening.

The horse or pony doing little other than gentle hacking will suffice on hay, supplemented with bran, chaff and nuts. But the mount that is hunted is going to need extra protein in body building foods such as oats and barley.

Remember, however, that horses are individuals. Like humans one may put on weight at the drop of a hat while another on the same rations may resemble a clothes hanger. So always check with a veterinarian if in doubt. Also bear in mind that the horse kept at grass will need supplementary feeding in the form of hay from November through to May, when there is no longer any goodness in the grass and, like its stabled companions, a little hard feed if it is asked to do extra work. Check daily in winter that the horse's water supply has not frozen. In intemperate climates it is advisable to provide a field shelter for the horse kept at grass, if you can or, at any rate, a New Zealand rug, which is made of weatherproof canvas and will protect it from the elements. The stabled horse which is clipped out, in other words, that has had its winter coat removed with electric clippers, must always be well rugged up with blankets and stable rugs. The following tack list gives the basic equipment that you will need.

Tack

Bridle and bit (with reins)
Saddle (i.e. with stirrup leathers and irons)
Numnah (Pad worn under saddle to prevent pressure on horse's back)
New Zealand rug
Stable rug
Blankets
Sweat rug (for use after strenuous exercise)

NB: When buying a horse or pony, its tack is often included in the purchase price, or can be separately negotiated.

Grooming equipment
Body brush for general use
Curry comb
Dandy brush (mud brush)
Hoof pick
Mane comb
Sponge
Box for grooming kit
First Aid kit
Hoof oil and brush

For the yard
Wheelbarrow
Fork
Spade
Buckets

Stable
Feed and water
buckets
Hay net and/or rack
Salt lick holder
Saddle rack (if not in tack room)

NB Your first aid kit will, of course, contain wound powder. Check your horse over very carefully when grooming for any sign of injury, for instance, he may have caught himself in some barbed wire.

Short Glossary of Terms

Bandages Used to protect a horse's legs and tail, particularly when travelling.

Bit Forms part of bridle. Regulates pace through the reins.

Buck Bad habit. Horse lowers head, arches back, leaps with all feet off the ground.

Cavesson Type of head collar used in breaking.

Colt Male foal under 4 years.

Colic Disease of digestive organs.

Condition Horse's health and general appearance.

Dressage Demonstrations of obedience of a horse.

Droppings Dung.

Farrier Person who shoes horses.

Filly Female foal under 4 years.

Girth Wide band which holds saddle in position — also describes the horse's middle.

Grazing Pasture where horses eat. Grazing land.

Gymkhana Horse and Pony Show with mounted games.

Hand Horse measurement of 4 inches (10cm).

Hogging Mane clipped short.

Horse box Vehicle for horse transportation.

Jodphurs Riding trousers, usually worn with boots, and always with regulation hard hat.

Laminitis Inflammation or fever of the feet.

Loose box Individual stable where horse has freedom of movement unlike stall in which it is tethered.

Mount A horse or pony for riding. (To mount a horse/mounting block etc.)

Muck-heap Manure heap.

Saddle soap Product for cleaning saddlery.

Tack Saddlery.

Tack room Where saddles and associated equipment are kept.

Trekking Covering long distances on horseback, usually at walking pace.

NB: Horses need regular worming. Anti-tetanus inoculations are also advisable. It is suggested that readers talk to their veterinarian about these, and other health matters.

Learning to Ride

Many a fearless rider will tell you that he was put on a pony as a child, made to remount when he fell off, and that he has never had a lesson in his life. Conversely, two good friends of mine, who ride extremely well, have been having — and enjoying — a weekly riding lesson for the past thirty years.

The aim of the majority, however, is to sustain sufficient confidence, balance and expertise, to enable them to sit a horse at the walk, trot, canter and gallop — hopefully jumping a bit — and, at the same time, making it as easy on their mount as possible, not bouncing about in the saddle like a sack of potatoes or jabbing at its bit, causing the animal pain. Indeed the lightest possible touch should be applied to get the best results and, in watching the world's best horsemen, you will see that use of the aids is almost indiscernible.

Before contemplating buying a horse or pony it is certainly advisable to have had the best tuition possible at a recommended riding school — in the United Kingdom one that is recognised by the British Horse Society.

Methods of tuition vary. Some instructors take pupils out for a hack, on quiet roads, or across the fields, from the outset, controlling the beginner's horse with a leading rein; others confine pupils to an indoor school until they have come to grips with the basics, that is, when they can mount and dismount, sit comfortably in the saddle, hodling the reins correctly, and can control their mount at its various paces.

The horse is controlled by the Aids, the body, seat, hands and voice. Whips and spurs are artificial Aids.

Light control is kept on the horse's mouth by use of the reins. Loosen this contact and the horse will quicken its paces. Sit down in the saddle, apply slight pressure on the reins and the horse will slow down. Use of the left rein in conjunction with light pressure from the right leg will tell the horse or pony to move to the left. The reverse instruction, and he will move to the right.

Changing from a walk to a trot, sit well down in the saddle, shorten your reins slightly, squeezing slightly behind the girth with your legs, and urge the pony on with your seat. Grip the saddle with your knees — keep your heels down.

Rising to the trot (Posting) is the hardest pace for the rider to master. This is a two-beat pace during which the rider rises up and down in the saddle making use of the stirrups.

I always associate this action with the traditional clip-clop sound, rising in the saddle on the clip, sitting down again on the clop. But this does take a little time to master. Once learnt it is never forgotten.

Cantering is more of a rocking horse movement in which the rider sits well down in the saddle.

The Gallop is the fastest pace of the horse, in effect a faster canter, but the pace is four-time and the sequence of the supporting legs is different.

Balance, when riding, is all important. It is something that comes with experience. So too does the ability to anticipate one's horse's actions before they occur and to be ready to check them.

Nowadays many people go on pony trekking holidays and this is an excellent introduction to riding for pleasure.

Equine Activities

Once you have been riding for a while there are many equine activities that you may wish to pursue ranging from competing at local gymkhanas in both ridden and in-hand classes to dressage competitions, driving, hunting, long distance riding, show jumping and western riding. You may develop an interest in racing or even aspire to playing polo. Young riders usually become members of the Pony Club. This was founded in 1929 to encourage young people to ride and enjoy sport connected with horses and ponies and to receive skilled instruction. Branches are to be found in most English-speaking countries.

In the *Almanac* you will find a number of references to High School horses, those trained in accordance with the principles of the classical art of riding practised in the European Courts in the mid-18th century. The skills are preserved and practised up to date, in the highest perfection, by the Spanish Riding School in Vienna with the famous white Lipizzaner stallions. Sometimes it is possible to watch their demonstrations in other countries of the world.

Generally training is started with the 'Piaffe', a cadenced trot on the spot, and this is used to develop the 'Passage' or 'Spanish Trot', when the horse rises off the ground energetically and throws forward the diagonal pair of legs. This is often followed by the 'Pirouette', a canter circling the inner hind leg — a very difficult exercise. These exercises are known as 'Schools on the Ground' and are sometimes required of riders at dressage competitions.

'Schools Above the Ground' are taught only at the Spanish Riding School. Only a few stallions are strong enough to perform these movements and a good indication of whether a horse is suitable, is work on the short rein. These movements are based on the 'Piaffe'. In the 'Pesade' the horse raises his forelegs, so that his body is balanced at an angle of 45 degrees to the ground, his forelegs are pulled closer to the chest and the hindlegs are pulled right up underneath the belly, supporting the horse's weight. In the 'Levade' the entire weight is shifted to the hindquarters and the haunches are bent even more sharply. Next is the 'Courbette', a series of forward jumps performed in the Levade position. Watching a demonstration of such skills is truly breathtaking.

Useful Addresses

Animal Health Trust
PO Box 5, Newmarket, Suffolk CB8 7DW

Anglo-Austrian Society
46, Queen Anne's Gate, London SW1 9AU

Association of British Riding Schools
Old Brewery Yard, Penzance, Cornwall TR18 2SL

Barend Riding and Trekking Centre
Sandyhills, By Dalbeattie, Dumfries and Galloway, Scotland

Bransby Home of Rest for Horses
Bransby, Saxilby, Lincoln LN1 2PH

The British Horse Society
British Equestrian Centre, Kenilworth, Warwick-shire CV8 2LR
(The British Horse Society is also the address for The Pony Club, The British Show Jumping Association and Riding for the Disabled).

British Show Pony Society
124 Green End Road, Sawtry, Huntingdon, Cambridgeshire

The British Lipizzaner Breeding Centre
Starrock Stud, Ludwell, Shaftesbury, Dorset SP7 0PW

The British Lipizzaner Horse Society
Ausdan Stud, Glynarthen, Llandysul, Dyfed SA44 6PB

The British Veterinary Association
7 Mansfield Street, London W1M 0AT

Horses and Ponies Protection Society
Greenbank Farm, Greenbank Drive, Fence, Nr Burnley, Lancs BB12 19QJ

Horse and Pony Rescue
(Mrs Lynn Philpott) 1 Milwards Cottages, Laughton,
Nr Lewes, East Sussex, BN8 6BN
(Please telephone early morning, or after dark, 0323
811254)

Horse and Pony Insurance (DBI)
Reference 267825, St Stephen's Court, St Stephen's
Road, Bournemouth, Dorset BH2 6LG

The Society for Companion Animal Studies
1a Hilton Road, Milngavie, Glasgow G62 7DN

There is a club for most horse breeds. The address of
the current secretary can, in most cases, be obtained
from the British Horse Society.

Overseas
Pony Clubs Association of Western Australia
13 Violet Ground, Shenton Park, Western Australia
6008

Canadian Pony Society
387 Hay Street, Woodstock, Ontario, N4S 2C5

(It is advisable to enclose a self-addressed stamped
envelope — in the case of overseas addresses, an
international reply coupon — when writing request-
ing information.)

Publications

Horse and Hound
King's Reach Tower, Stamford Street,
London SE1 9LS

Horse and Pony
Bretton Court, Bretton, Peterborough PE3 8DZ

Horse and Rider
296 Ewell Road, Surbiton, Surrey KT6 7AD

Pony
(as *Horse and Rider*)